THE AUTOBIOGRAPHY

AND

MEMORIALS OF

CAPTAIN OBADIAH CONGAR.

FOR

FIFTY YEARS MARINER AND SHIPMASTER FROM THE PORT OF NEW YORK.

BY REV. HENRY T. CHEEVER,

AUTHOR OF

"THE ISLAND WORLD OF THE PACIFIC," AND "THE WHALE AND HIS CAPTORS."

He is careful in observing the Lord's day. He hath a watch in his heart, though no bells in a steeple to proclaim that day by ringing to prayers. He daily sees and duly considers God's wonders in the deep. —FULLER'S "*Good Sea Captain.*"

NEW YORK.

HARPER & BROTHERS, PUBLISHERS,

82 CLIFF STREET.

1851.

PREFACE.

To the mass of general readers, and to earnest minds especially, writings in the shape of self-memorial and autobiography are always attractive. Whether they be purely religious, like the Confessions of Augustine, or the Grace Abounding of the Immortal Dreamer, or the Experiences of Madame Guyon and of Cowper; or whether they be semi-religious, literary, and economical, like the Life of Franklin, by himself, the Confessions of Rousseau, the Autobiographies of Goëthe and Leigh Hunt, or the Confidences of Lamartine, all men love to read them. Personal reminiscences, perhaps it may be added, even egotism, we are generally eager to peruse when written, although we detest and can not bear them when spoken.

It is because I have thought there is something here of universal interest—because I have seemed to see that, in the workings and struggles, the trials and triumphs of the SAILOR herein exhibited, there is matter for thought and instruction to the Man, certainly to the Christian every where—it is for this, among other reasons, that the Editor has undertaken the task (not an easy one) of correcting, reducing, fashioning, and putting them in order.

The labor expended in this process, if not always the same in kind, has been little less in amount than that of creating entire a similar book. But the work has been lightened by the hope that its result may now and then profitably occupy a captain's lonely hours at sea, or a sailor's dog-watch and Sunday, and that it may minister healthful stimulus and nutrition to a circle of minds on the shore also, earnestly longing after holiness.

In now giving this work to the world, the Editor remembers the charge of Carlyle: Cast forth thy act—thy word into the ever-living universe: it is a seed-grain that can not die; unnoticed to-day, it may be found flourishing as a banyan grove after a thousand years. If this book shall enter as aliment or as vital electricity into but one upright mind, so as to make it more resolved and holy, and its action more quick and powerful for good on other minds, a wave of benign influence will have been started by it, humble as it is, that shall roll through eternity.

In the hope that this volume may prove a useful gift to the Merchant Service and Marine of England and America, it is now dedicated to the Seamen's Friend Societies of the two great COMMERCIAL NATIONS, whose common boast it is

"That Chatham's language is their mother tongue."

HENRY T. CHEEVER.

New York, January, 1851.

CONTENTS.

CHAPTER I.

INTRODUCTORY AND GENERAL VIEW OF CHARACTER.

CHAPTER II.

EARLY VOYAGES, SUFFERINGS, ADVENTURES, PERILS, AND ESCAPES.

CHAPTER III.

RELIGIOUS CONVICTIONS, PROVIDENCES, TRIALS, AND TRIUMPHS.

CHAPTER IV.

RELIGIOUS EXPERIENCE, PROFESSION, TEMPTATIONS, AND ESCAPE.

CHAPTER V.

NAVIGATING FOR ETERNITY. LIGHTS AND SHADOWS OF THE CHRISTIAN LIFE.

CHAPTER VI.

LABORS WITH HIMSELF AND LABORS IN BEHALF OF THE SABBATH FOR SEAMEN.

CHAPTER VII.

CHRISTIAN LIFE AND DUTIES AT SEA CONTINUED.

CHAPTER VIII.

PECULIAR RELIGIOUS EXERCISES AND ORIGINAL CORRESPONDENCE WITH REV. THOMAS SCOTT.

CHAPTER IX.

DESPONDENCY CONFESSED, CORRECTED, AND CURED.

CHAPTER X.

ABANDONMENT OF THE SEA. TRAVELS AND EXPERIENCE IN THE SOUTHWEST.

CHAPTER XI.

BUSINESS, BENEVOLENCE, AND MENTAL EXERCISES ON SHORE CONTINUED.

CHAPTER XII.

LIFE, LABORS, AND EXPERIENCE AT JACKSONVILLE.

CHAPTER XIII.

CLOSING YEARS, DEATH, AND RETROSPECT OF CHARACTER.

MEMOIRS

OF

CAPTAIN CONGAR.

CHAPTER I.

INTRODUCTORY AND GENERAL VIEWS OF CHARACTER.

I COME not, friends, to steal away your hearts;
But, as you know me all, a plain, blunt man.
For I have neither wit, nor words, nor worth,
Action, nor utterance, nor the power of speech,
To stir men's blood; I only speak right on;
I tell you that which you yourselves do know.

SHAKSPEARE'S *Julius Cæsar*.

THE subject of the following memoir was the fourth of seven children born to David and Mary Congar, and all reared to adult years. He was born near Newark, New Jersey, on the 27th of June, 1768. His death was in July, 1848, in the eighty-second year of his age. His parentage, though poor, was virtuous, industrious, temperate, pious, and long-lived; the father dying at the age of eighty-seven, the mother at seventy-nine.

He was sent to school, for one or two years, at the age of six, just before the commencement of the American Revolution; at the breaking out of which, his father's family were removed up the North River, to the village of New Windsor, sixty miles from the city of New York, in the year 1776. Here Obadiah was taken on board a sloop by his father, who had abandoned the business of shoe-making in order to follow that of a coaster and trader on the Hudson. By this means the son early acquired a knowledge of nautical life, and contracted a fondness for the water.

About the year 1779, however, his father sold his river craft, and took up the business of ferry-keeping, using also his young sailor-son to go with him. This had nearly been a fatal business for them both; for it happened, on a Sabbath day, that they had occasion to take on board a heavy-loaded wagon and five horses, and having gone about midchannel, that is, half a mile from the shore, the wind blowing fresh from the southwest and ebb tide, which caused considerable swell, the horses sallied to leeward, and the boat immediately filled and sunk, all except a little part of the bow, to which they all providentially clung, and remained until taken off. Happily for them, this disaster happened just as the church doors were opened for the people to come out, and, being in full view, assistance was soon rendered them.

This narrow escape from drowning, which was but one of many he met with in the course of life, wrought powerfully upon the mind of the boy-mariner. It led him, beyond what was natural to his years, to think of his liability to die, and of the necessity of being always ready. And it seems to have given birth to many good resolutions, and to have laid a strong arm of restraint upon youthful follies, making him serious-minded and afraid of sin, lest God should snatch him away in the commission of it.

When about fourteen years of age, his father wisely attempted to put him to a trade; but, finding the lad not to take readily to any of the mechanic arts, he thought proper to send him to school for the purpose of learning navigation, in order that he might follow the sea for life. Soon after he had thus acquired the theory of navigation, which there is good evidence that he mastered well, the contest ended between the United States and Great Britain, and he entered a vessel as a common hand in the coasting business.

Through sundry imprudences and prodigality incident to his age, he found himself, on settling with his first employers, and proceeding to the city of New York, in the winter of 1785, quite out of pocket. He notes this as a providential circumstance, because, probably, his poverty kept him out of harm's way during his stay in the city; and, reflecting upon his previous sailor-like improvidence, he wisely resolved to husband his earnings better for the future, a resolution which, if carried out by young sailors generally as it was by him, would early lay the foundation of an independent competence.

It was at this period of his life, in the eighteenth year thereof, and with a serious though not yet a religious mind, that the personal narrative or journal was undertaken from which the materials of this book are derived. It was principally, he says, that he might retain or call to mind the most material incidents of his life, the perusal of which might be useful and entertaining, should he ever arrive at old age. It is written in a legible, fair hand, and with generally correct orthography; and though by no means remarkable for the shrewdness and originality of its observations, or the depth of its reflections, or the animation and interest of its style, or the lively detail of stirring facts, incidents, and adventures, it is, on the whole, highly creditable to the heart, if not to the intellect of the writer; and it presents an example every way worthy of imitation by sea-faring men.

The character it gradually develops is the rare one of a humble, conscientious, active, and practical Christian mariner. Without being eminently great or transcendently good, it is such a character as, if every where reproduced and multiplied on ship and shore, would make society happy, and earth akin to heaven. It is a character the ground-work of which is altogether natural and common, being neither much above nor any below the ordinary level of human abilities, but so ribbed, braced, and undergirded by strong moral principle and the fear of God, that it was far more than ordinarily effective for good in its day and generation. Thence alone it is worthy of study and imitation by those especially whose sphere of action and duty corresponds to that pursued by the practical Christian mariner herein exemplified. There are few that attain to the office of shipmaster, like Captain Congar, who might not become as respected, influential, and useful as he, provided only they had his religion, which was the rudder of his life.

One of his personal friends and acquaintances, a New York merchant, who first knew him as long ago as the year 1808, in Newark, thus testifies to Captain Congar's character, person, and worth: "I observed him always as a serious-minded man. When in port, he was sure to be seen regularly and punctually in his seat at church on the Sabbath, and also at social evening meetings; and he always enjoyed the respect and confidence of the better class of society.

"He was a man of a middle size, rather spare or slender, neat and particular in his dress, and this he retained to the end of his days. He had a little hesitancy in his speech, and a nervous habit of shutting his eyes suddenly and often while speaking. Though inclined to be irritable in temper, he always maintained his Christian character, and was at peace with all men.

"Captain Congar was in the employ of some of our best and most respectable merchants, and had their full confidence; and though their views of sending out ships from port on the Sabbath differed from the captain's, they seemed to yield to his sense of Christian duty. Captain Congar was an old-fashioned Christian, and of the Puritan stamp; he could not bear deceit nor equivocation, was scrupulous as to his engagements, and opposed to being in debt.

"My particular acquaintance with him was after his removal to Florida, to which place he removed on account of climate, and with reference to his health. He established himself at St. Augustine in mercantile business to rather a limited extent, had capital sufficient to pay for a stock of goods suited to the place, to own a house and lot, and was also cultivating a young orange grove, which bade fair to yield a considerable income, when the severe frost of (about) 1835 destroyed it, and it was not afterward replenished or improved.

"Captain Congar was too candid and honest, and too cautious to gain much by trade in those times of over-reaching and exaggeration. He was particular to purchase only good articles, and was undeviating in prices. The common people, the Monorcans, and the poor slaves, found the benefit of trading at his store; and if he recommended his goods, they could believe him, and were sure not to be deceived.

"At St. Augustine Captain Congar was forward in efforts to erect a place of worship and support a church, and to promote good morals, always bore his part liberally in the support of the Gospel, was regular and systematic in his benevolence. He was in the habit of remitting his contributions to the seamen's cause, to the

American Board of Commissioners for Foreign Missions, and other public charities, and he adorned his profession by a consistent life.

"Captain Congar became dissatisfied with St. Augustine, and at the advanced age of seventy commenced a new residence at Jacksonville, in Florida, in 1838. Here he opened a store, and for several years did a small amount of trade, but gradually withdrew from business pursuits. He was chosen Mayor of Jacksonville, and exerted a strong influence for the sacredness of the Sabbath, and in opposition to intemperance, profane swearing, gambling, and all public wickedness.

"He began at once to propose plans for a Church organization and to procure a church edifice, and though he did not succeed in permanently establishing a Church and place of worship for his own denomination, he yielded his own preference, and cordially united in aid of an Evangelical Methodist Church, which continues to be respectably attended, and is regularly supplied with preaching. He also erected, with the aid of a few friends, a house for prayer, on the same lot in Jacksonville with his own dwelling, and kept up evening prayer meetings by his personal efforts for a considerable time.

"While at Jacksonville in the winter of 1849, I learned much of Captain Congar's catholic spirit, and his efforts to keep a high standard of Christian example. He used to look after members who were delinquent at the evening prayer meetings, and his influence in every way was corrective and salutary."

Perhaps the noblest attitude in which the subject of these memoirs appears, is the firm and manly stand taken by him in respect to the observance of the Sabbath at sea. It is in this pre-eminently that his example is to be commended to all the craft. When there were none of his fellow-captains to keep him in countenance, he maintained rigidly, by practice and precept, the sanctity of the Lord's day, so that he would neither sail from port, nor have any other than the absolutely necessary working of the ship at sea.

This he conscientiously held to for the whole of his sea life, after embracing Christianity, when scarce another could be quoted in England or America who was with him; and even grave divines, as will be seen, demurred at giving the counsel which he prescribed to himself, and for a length of years never deviated from. Out of forty-seven voyages performed by him in all, during the twenty-three that he was himself captain, he had the Sabbath carefully observed to the best of his ability by all on board. For this we honor him; for this, if for nothing else, his life were worthy to be written; for this, while the name of the wicked shall rot, his shall be had in everlasting remembrance. Forasmuch as he honored the Sabbath when by others it was dishonored, the great God of the Sabbath shall make him honorable in the everlasting kingdom of our Lord, agreeably to that word of his, *Them that honor me I will honor, but they that despise me shall be lightly esteemed.*

In the following chapters of this book we shall have Captain Congar speak as much as possible for himself, without, however, presenting his journal in due order or exactness, but omitting many things inconsequential and uninteresting, paraphrasing others, and so abridging both incidents and reflections, and condensing the whole, as to bring the volume within the compass we have prescribed for it.

Although a man noted for uncommon humility, self-distrust, and freedom from egotism, Captain Congar surmised and hoped, in his last days, that the perusal of his journal might be useful to others, and he therefore left it by will as a legacy to the Seamen's Friend Society, with instructions to have a book prepared out of it, and three thousand copies to be printed and circulated among seamen at his expense. The present volume is in fulfillment of that trust.

The aim of the editor has been so to project his own mind into the position and character of the subject of this memoir, as from that stand-point to trace a true map of his life and religious experience. May it prove a valuable addition to the Christian literature of the sea, and in due time find its way to forecastle and cabin, and be a monitor and example to officers and men, of modest worth and principle, and of the honor that accrues, even in this world, to real goodness and the fear of God. Should it ever, in a good degree, answer this end, or might it serve as a new REVOLVING LIGHT to the mariner on the look-out for the Port of Peace, the labors of the editor will have been well bestowed. On its mission, then, he sends it forth, with an earnest prayer to God for every mariner that shall ever be allured to its perusal.

DARK is the watery way
  Of life's tempestuous sea;
And none, oh Christ, are safe, but they
  Who put their trust in thee.

Loud is the stormy wind;
  The seamen are afraid;
But those shall strength and mercy find
  Whose souls on Christ are stayed.

The winds THEY do not fear,
  Nor dread the thunder's noise;
The Savior's cheering voice THEY hear,
  And evermore rejoice.
It is our Savior's skill,
  Our Savior's arm of might,
Which guides the tossing ship at will,
  And puts our fears to flight.

Praise to the Pilot's power,
  Praise to the Pilot's hand,
That, faithful most in danger's hour,
  Shall bring us safe to land.

CHAPTER II.

EARLY VOYAGES, SUFFERINGS, ADVENTURES, PERILS, AND ESCAPES.

WE have been
But voyaging along the barren coasts,
Like some poor, ever-roaming horde of pirates,
Who, crowded in the rank and narrow ship,
House on the wild sea with wild usages,
Nor know aught of the main land, but the bays
Where safeliest they may venture a thief's landing.
The Piccolomini.

THE first cruise made by Captain Congar off soundings was from New York to North Carolina, in a sloop, in the year 1785. Though but a seven or eight days' sail, it was a trading voyage, and occupied six months. At first, in his extreme distress by sea-sickness, he made to himself the sailor's usual promise, that, could he once more get on land, salt water should never again wet his feet. But, returning with good success, and greeted joyfully by his friends, a few days on land sufficed him, and, refusing the owner's offer to take the sloop on shares and continue in the river business, he resolved to pursue his fortune on the sea.

The taste he had had of its dangers and discomforts did not appall him, although he records afterward the following reminiscence of his first voyage, in order to show what dreadful apprehensions fill the mind when guilt stares in the face, and when some awful judgment seems to threaten. While his sloop was lying at the mouth of one of the Carolina rivers, the captain had occasion to take all the crew ashore with him but young Congar, late in the afternoon, and, by some means, they were detained all night. As the vessel lay about half a mile from land, it was but natural that the raw sailor boy left in charge should feel lonesome and uneasy. But his fund of spirits and health helped him, and he endeavored to compose his mind to sleep at the usual hour.

About midnight, as he deemed, he was awakened by the great rocking of the vessel, and by loud peals of thunder, terrifying to him at any time, but now, in his loneliness, distressing beyond measure: "The vivid lightnings flashed around me as though the elements were all on fire. What horror seized my guilty soul! Now I tried to pray; now I read the Bible. Now I repented of my sins, and resolved to mend my ways. I thought the judgment day had come, and that my soul must perish. In this dreadful time I had, nevertheless, presence of mind enough to go on deck and let go the second anchor, and try the pump. After this, it moderated a little, but I thought the night would never end. Blessed be God, who carried me through that dreadful night, and gave me to see the light and space to repent!"

Eager again for the sea, and all its terrors out of mind, in an evil hour for himself, young Congar enlisted on board an English vessel bound to the island of St. Vincent's, in the West Indies. During this voyage he "suffered almost every thing but death itself," the vessel being ill commanded and provisioned, and quite unfit for sea, so that they were very soon put upon a short allowance of bread and water; the captain, withal, being, by his description, "an inhuman tyrant, who knew not how to treat any being capable of feeling."

After the lapse of forty-seven wearisome days of hunger, thirst, and hard usage, they made port, the captain, by the imperfect navigation of the time, having fallen so far to leeward as to have to stand to the northward again, in order to make an easting. Such was the inhumanity of the captain, that the men were put upon allowance again only eight days after getting to port, and so remained for eight or ten weeks, to the end of the voyage.

The whole course of it was so fraught with hardship, that at its close and return to New York, nothing seemed wanting to young Congar but opportunity to engage in some calling whereby he might earn an honest livelihood, and be delivered from the toils of the seas. This was offered him in a clerkship at Newark, in a merchant's store. But finding the business dull and the confinement irksome, and his sufferings at sea being all forgotten, he abandoned it at the expiration of eighteen months for a home again on the mountain wave, a life which he had but lately detested as the most uncomfortable to be imagined.

Reflecting thereon at a later period, he remarks, "Would any one seriously reflect how many comforts of life he deprives himself of by following the sea, methinks all the allurements to such a business would vanish. But few, alas! regard what ought to be esteemed the greatest comfort—I mean, the privilege of living under a preached Gospel, or being in habits of sociability with those whose examples of piety and virtue might lead to a consideration of the importance of preparing for our latter end—considerations seemingly too much neglected by those whose occupation is on the great waters."

His clerkship had hardly been mòre productive than trading before on the North River, so that he started anew for sea in his nineteenth year without even the means of procuring an outfit. Through the kindness of his late employer, this, however, was furnished him, and he shipped as a common sailor for a voyage to Jamaica, but upon such hard conditions, and as a supernumerary hand, that nothing was due him at the winding up of the voyage.

A painful melancholy had preyed upon him on the voyage, which was rather increased by the uncertainty of his prospects, and the difficulty of finding employment that suited him on his return. At length, however, it was relieved through the services of a friend procuring him a situation in a brig to Guadaloupe on seamen's wages. This was a prosperous voyage, with an honest captain, that did much to reconcile him to the rough life of a sailor. But on his return to Newburyport in January, and a voyage afterward in February to New York of twenty-six days, he suffered all the rigors of an ice-bound coast.

We find him next embarked for Ireland, and returning by way of the Cape de Verds with a cargo of salt, and now thoroughly broken in to the rough and tumble of a sailor's life, and inured to all its vices. A cruise to St. Domingo and back to Newburyport completed the year 1788, in the course of which his vessel sprung a leak in a gale, and by working at the pumps he was fatigued to that degree that death seemed almost desirable, all unfit for it as he then was.

Being of a social turn at this age, and finding congeniality, a warm attachment seems to have been formed with the people of Newburyport, whom he began to esteem as fathers and brothers. "With them," he says, "I would go to church, and talk of religion too; but, though given up at the same time to all kinds of wickedness, yet I was not so lost to all future concern but that I bought me a Bible before I went to sea again." This was probably the result of some promise made when in distress on the last voyage.

In the chances and changes of a seaman's life, young Congar is next sick with a malignant fever at Port au Prince. Greatly alarmed and anxious, he spent much time in reflection on his past conduct, and frequently resolved, should he be spared, to amend his ways and become a Christian. But, like thousands of seamen in the same distress, health no sooner returned than all such thoughts were banished from his mind. Through God's mercy he was saved, and we find him successively after at Newburyport, Norfolk, London, and Orient France, enlarging his knowledge of the great world, but, as himself frequently confesses, ill preparing for the world to come: "All this while I was daily becoming more and more hardened in sin; I chose to follow the multitude to do evil, and scarcely ever looked into my new Bible. Nevertheless, the force of education was so great, that at times I would attempt to pray. But, God knows, my prayers needed forgiveness."

In December of 1789, he being now in the twenty-second year of his age, and evidently a trusty seaman, proposals were made him to go in a brig in the capacity of a first mate. With some reluctance, and an unfeigned diffidence of his own abilities, he assumed the berth. But, owing to difficulties with his men, partly consequent upon his own conscientiousness, he enters in his diary that sometimes he would willingly have given up his officership, with all its cares and troubles, and all the profits attached to it, and have returned to the capacity of a sailor again, rather than be continually at war with those under his direction.

His first foreign voyage as mate to Cowes, in

the Isle of Wight, and Bremen, Germany, was a harassing and disastrous one, by reason of dreadful storms, length of passage, injury to cargo, and the loss of some of his men, and the reduction to short allowance of bread, beef, and water. On the 16th of August, 1790, being bound from Bremen to Charleston, they came to one and a half biscuit per day, and, to make the water serve, he enters in his journal, "we used to put a quill in a bottle and drink through it, and thereby quench thirst without using so much as we must otherwise have done. By this time, great prospect of our suffering with hunger began to appear, we being a long way from any land, and in the calm latitudes. Every countenance began to wear the aspect of concern; for my part, the unpleasant situation in which we were placed caused many serious reflections in my mind. I viewed it as the judgment of an avenging God pursuing me wherever I went. But, alas! for all this my heart was not truly humbled. Nevertheless, I thought it was my duty, and, as I had often resolved, I now attempted to set about a new life; but religion which has no foundation but the fear of present and future evil will not likely be very lasting. Impressed at this time with a sense of my dependence on God, I wrote the following prayer, that it might remain an evidence how seriously my mind was affected with our situation. Monday forenoon. — O, most gracious Father and Lord, be pleased to look down from thy holy habitation, and have mercy upon us miserable creatures. Forgive us our manifold sins and transgressions, which from time to time we have committed against thy divine majesty. And O, merciful Saviour, visit us with the smiles of thy blessed grace, that we may not only forsake our evil ways, which we have been pursuing all our lives past, but that we may be renewed by thy good Spirit, and be enabled to live more agreeably to thy holy will henceforward.

"Most gracious and merciful God, as it hath pleased thee to preserve us, from time to time, upon the raging seas, and to hold our life even when we expected to be swallowed up of the merciless ocean, so likewise be pleased of thine infinite goodness at this time to extend thy mercy toward us guilty creatures, and let us not perish under thy bountiful hand. Grant us favorable winds, O Lord, that we may be delivered from our troubles, and be brought to our desired port. And O, heavenly Father, give us hearts ever thankful to thee for all thy goodness toward us unworthy sinners, and that we may ever bless and praise thy holy name, give all honor to thee who art ever just and righteous, for the sake of thy dear Son, Savior of the world. Amen.

"On the evening of the same day there sprung up a breeze to the eastward, which gave us a run on our passage. And Providence designed, to lessen our troubles still more, that we might see his power in the deep, and be led to adore his condescending goodness to the worst of sinners. The next evening we spoke a Portuguese ship from the coast of Brazil bound to Lisbon. We went on board of her and got about one hundred and fifty pounds of rice, one barrel of cassada meal, eight pounds of sugar, and about ten pounds of pork, which articles were of great use to us, and relieved our distresses in a great measure.

"About this time, in opening the Bible, I took particular notice of these words in Isaiah: 'Behold, the Lord's hand is not shortened that it can not save, neither his ear heavy that it can not hear.' This led me to admire the providence of God in stretching forth his hand to save them that are ready to perish, and hearing those that call on him in time of trouble. For these mercies I seemed truly thankful, and promised a reformation of life; and had I sought to him whose hand is not shortened that it can not save, perhaps I might have been enabled to fulfill this promise in some measure; but, putting confidence in my own strength and abilities, my resolutions proved like the morning cloud, or the early dew when the sun is risen.

"From the time we spoke the Portuguese ship until we saw another sail was nearly twenty days, in which time our distresses would have greatly increased had we not met with the above relief. When we arrived at Charleston, we had not any provisions at all for more than six days. September 13th we made the light-house, and the same day, with much difficulty, got into port. I returned thanks to God for his special mercies toward us in preserving us when want and famine, with all its awful consequences, seemed to threaten us, and for restoring us to our desired port once more in safety. But, nevertheless, my heart was far alienated from God.

"I had often resolved while at sea, if we should arrive safe, that I would leave the brig, and return home to my native place, having been some time from it, but the captain not being willing to part with me, I concluded to go another voyage. We were employed taking in our cargo and getting ready for sea until the

6th of October, when we sailed for the island of St. Martin's. This voyage was principally undertaken with the view to bring back a cargo of salt. From the time we sailed until November 1st nothing extraordinary happened. Being then in the latitude of Barbuda, a small island to the eastward of St. Martin's, at eight o'clock in the evening we hove our ship to under the two top-sails, with her head to the southward, supposing, by our observation, to be something to the southward of the island, and by this means we could not drift on to it. At midnight we could not observe any thing like land, nor any appearance of the water being colored. At one A.M., it being dark, but pretty moderate, the first thing we knew, the vessel struck upon rocks, which soon brought us upon deck, and in great confusion, for we soon observed rocks on every side, and some above the water. Directly after we discovered land, and, to our astonishment, to the southward of us. We used every endeavor to get clear, but all to no purpose, except that we got our vessel in such a situation that she could not sink entirely under water. Finding every attempt to get off fail us, we let go an anchor, hove out the long boat, and sounded for the best water. At daylight we carried out a kedge anchor, and hove upon it, but in vain; and about seven A.M. she bilged, and, being most water forward, her bows sunk entirely under, but her stern was kept up by rocks which she had got fast upon.

"Circumstanced as we were, it is highly reasonable to conclude we must all have perished had the wind blown fresh from the northward. I count this deliverance among the many providential escapes from threatening death which I have experienced, and for which I desire to be truly thankful. At eight A.M., finding the leak increasing fast upon us, we left the pumps, and endeavored to save what we could with our boat. The first load we took on shore was our clothing, and some provisions and water, not knowing that either of these things, or even inhabitants, were to be found there, the island appearing barren and wild. This island lies in the latitude of eighteen degrees north, and about the longitude of sixty-one and a half west. The whole island (being small) belongs to a gentleman in England, who has an overseer or governor upon it, who manages his business. This governor has one white overseer under him, and about one hundred slaves, whose business chiefly is to raise stock and carry it to Antigua, which lies about thirty miles to the southward of Barbuda. There are kept here two small vessels, which carry the produce of the island to the aforesaid place, and also two large boats, rowed by fourteen hands, which are sent to the assistance of those whose lot it may be to get on these rocks, which almost surround the island.

"When the boat landed, some negroes who were near the place came and conducted the captain to the governor's house, where he remained until next morning, and ordered the boat on board, with directions to load her again with the most valuable articles, and all to come on shore, which we did, and landed a little before dark. The next morning we all went on board again, and endeavored to save what we could, and brought it on shore, where we remained the second night; and the day following, returning on board, we brought every thing which it was possible to save.

"November 5th, we sailed with the effects of the wreck for Antigua, where we arrived the next day, and the effects, being landed, were sold at auction, when we received our wages, and every one took what course he thought proper. I took passage for the island of Guadaloupe, in hopes to meet with some vessel for New York; but, not finding any, I proceeded to St. Eustatia, and from thence to St. Martin's, where I fell in with the sloop Arabia, Captain Johnson, bound for New York, who offered me a passage, which I willingly accepted. We sailed November 28th, and, after a passage of twenty-one days, arrived at New York.

"From thence I proceeded to Newark, to visit my relations and friends, having been absent from them about three years. I was received by my connections and acquaintance with marks of sincere congratulation, some of whom professed a great desire that I would quit the seafaring business, and undertake something on shore. But I had become too great a rover to listen to such entreaties. After spending a few days at Newark, I went to see my parents at New Windsor, whom I had not visited in five years, and who always had expressed great satisfaction on my returning from sea. I remained with them about ten days, when a letter was received from my brother at Newark that a Mr. S. wanted me to return and act as mate of a schooner which he was fitting out for North Carolina, and commanded by William Whitmore. To this I consented, and we sailed from New York February 3d, 1791, for Wilmington.

"I now began to throw off that watchfulness over my conduct and seeming duty to God which engaged my thoughts in times of distress, and had nearly forgotten all the promises I had made heretofore. And though I did not give way altogether to such gross acts of sin as I had been guilty of before, yet, it grieves me to say, I lived entirely in the neglect of every religious duty, and became more and more careless about my eternal welfare. How wonderful is the forbearance and long-suffering of God in sparing such guilty creatures. Surely it is because the Lord is God and not man that we are not consumed.

"We arrived at our desired port after a passage of twelve days, where we lay some time, and then proceeded for Charleston, South Carolina, and from thence to New York again, where we arrived the first of April, fitted out for the West Indies, and sailed the sixteenth for St. Thomas, an island belonging to the Danes. We reached it in safety, after a passage of twenty-five days, and lay about eight weeks discharging our cargo and taking in another.

"Being ready for sea, July 14th, we sailed for New York again, where we arrived after a moderate passage of twenty days. August 25th, I engaged on board the same vessel again for the purpose of fitting out with a cargo of horses for Port au Prince.

"By this time, I say it sorrowing, I had become, as it were, an abandoned reprobate, and had put off the fear of God from before my eyes. Why was I not cast off and plunged into the deepest hell? Why did the Almighty reach forth his hand and save me when, to all appearance, we were in imminent danger? To illustrate the mercy of God to me in a providential manner, I shall relate a circumstance which took place October 6th, being then in the latitude of twenty-seven degrees north, and longitude of sixty-six degrees west.

"Toward evening of the afore-mentioned day, it began to blow fresh, and came on very thick weather. Accordingly, we shortened sail. It continued to blow much the same, with excessive heavy rain and exceedingly dark, until about eleven P.M., when, all on a sudden, we were struck by a violent squall, which knocked us down on our beam ends, and, at the same time, all the hay that was upon the awning went overboard. Providentially for us, the horses had been well secured before night, so that none of them fetched away or broke loose. Had not this been the case, in all probability we should have been lost, for every thing in the cabin fell to leeward, and it was with great difficulty that the watch below got on deck. We lay in this condition about five minutes, in the course of which time we cut the main halyards and got the sail down. Upon this being done, she wore round, and having got her before the wind, she righted, and we continued to scud to the westward until daylight, when we hove to under a balanced main sail. In the after part of the day the wind shifted suddenly to the westward, attended with tremendous flashes of lightning, insomuch that the sea appeared as if it were all on fire, while the hoarse thunder followed, peal on peal, as though nature were about to give its last expiring groan.

"During this voyage in particular, I had become very profane, and had almost totally banished the fear of God from my mind. But, while lying in Port au Prince, I was seized with a fever, which brought me to reflect a little, so that I left the practice of swearing, and would sometimes attempt to pray. But those were prayers that needed forgiveness.

"We arrived at New York from Port au Prince December 18th, and, having discharged our cargo, I left the vessel, determining never to go another voyage with a load of live-stock; and as Mr. S. gave me to understand that he intended to put horses on board, I gave up all idea of proceeding in her, and on the twenty-fourth of said month went over to Newark, with an intention to remain at home through the winter, and study the French language, from an apprehension that it might be of signal service to me in the West India trade. I engaged in and continued my study, though not with the strictest attention, until the sixth of March, 1792. At this time, my teacher being taken sick, and having run through nearly all my money, I began to think it high time to go to sea again. Accordingly, I went over to New York with a view to look for a berth, and happening to fall in with an acquaintance who was going as second mate of the ship Nancy, Captain Wheaton, for Canton, in China, the voyage pleasing me, I engaged to go before the mast or otherwise, in the capacity of a sailor.

"Being about to undertake a voyage which would be longer than I had been accustomed to, I began to consider seriously what I had been doing, and to take myself to task for my past life. I had been living in a course of sin and neglect of religion for many months. Add to this, that I considered my time and money spent to little advantage while studying French. Once more, then, I resolved to quit my sinful habits, and live more conformably to that religion which I had been educated in. But, alas!

evil had become so rooted in my very nature, that nothing short of Almighty power could heal my corrupted heart, and enable me to tread the paths of virtue and piety.

"We had a very favorable passage to the island of St. Jago, one of the Cape de Verds, where we watered and replenished our stock, and sailed again on the sixteenth of April, and reached the Cape of Good Hope by the twenty-third of June. At this place are two roadsteads, one at Table Bay, which is the principal place at the Cape, and the other at False Bay, which lies on the southeast side of the promontory, and where ships ride from May until October. About this time the prevailing winds come from the southeast, and then ships go round to Table Bay until the May following.

"We lay at the Cape until July 11th, discharging part of our cargo and taking on board seal skins. Great part of the time we lay at this plaçe the winds blew exceedingly strong from the northwest quarter, which being favorable for us, we proceeded in due time on our way to Cânton. August 21st, we entered the Straits of Sunda. On the twenty-second we were off Ango Point, and several canoes came alongside with turtle, poultry, fruit, tortoise shell, walking-sticks, monkeys, birds, and a variety of curiosities. The land along here appeared very fertile, with abundance of cocoanut trees.

"The town at Ango Point is small and very compact, built with bamboo and covered with thatch, and inhabited by natives who are called Malays, an uncivilized and very savage people. The Malays are generally about five feet two or three inches high, not very stout made, and of a copper or tawny complexion. In the Straits of Malacca, and among all those islands, they frequently capture merchantmen, the crews of which they instantly put to death. These people make use of a composition called fanam, which they chew in order to make their teeth black.

"From the Straits of Sunda to Canton we had favorable winds, and on the thirteenth of September made the Grand Ladrone Island, and the same day came to anchor in Macao Roads. Macao is a considerable town, inhabited by the Chinese and Portuguese; but though it is partly garrisoned by the latter, yet they have but little to say respecting the police. They are the only nation who are entitled to the privilege of settling in China, this favor being granted them on account of their being the first navigators that found a passage from Europe to this great empire by water, thus opening the great trade now carried on from all parts of the world to this country.

"September 14th, we proceeded up to Wampoa, a small town about fourteen miles below Canton, and nearly one hundred from Macao. Here the shipping lie, there not being water sufficient for them to proceed further up. Thus, after a passage of nearly six months (including the time we lay at the Cape of Good Hope), we arrived at what the Chinese vaingloriously call the Celestial Empire, the distance being about twelve thousand miles from America.

"As I hinted at the commencement of this voyage, my mind took a religious turn again, and on the passage I had often formed resolutions to betake myself to such a course of life as would insure some happiness, having, upon mature consideration, come to this conclusion, that happiness was not to be found in a sinful course of life: thence the reason why I had never experienced any. Having much opportunity, my mind was much employed contemplating on these things. Yet, under these impressions, I could not see that beauty in religion that I would be willing to give up all for the sake of it; and though I had beheld many of the wonders of Providence, yet I could not take God for my portion.

"About a month after our arrival at Canton, a Captain Smith, who had sold his vessel in India, a Mr. Green, and Mr. Woods, who had been mates of vessels, had some business to Macao, and, as we were not much employed on board, they prevailed upon Captain Wheaton to let them take the ship's long boat and two hands to take them to the above-mentioned place, having with them two American sailors, one of them named Allen and the other Melvin, besides a Frenchman, who wished to take a passage with us.

"David Andress and myself were the two pitched upon for this expedition. We left the ship on Saturday, October 13th, 1792, at about one o'clock P.M., being eight in number. The wind being favorable, though but light, and the tide being with us, we passed through the Bogue of Tigris, which is about thirty-five miles from Canton, at eight P.M. We continued on as far as Green Island, and came to anchor about nine miles from the Bogue of Tigris, it being thought imprudent to run in the night, on account of the fishing stakes placed in different parts of the passage which leads from Canton to Macao. By means of a rope stretched from one to the other, about eight feet from the water, for the purpose of strengthening them, the passage is rendered very dangerous for small boats.

"Under an apprehension that these stakes might be fatal to us should we venture to run in the night, our gentlemen thought most prudent to come to anchor and wait for daylight. Now, however imprudent it might be to run while the tide was against us, it certainly was much more so with the tide in our favor. Nevertheless, our gentlemen became impatient, and, the wind springing up pretty fresh, they determined to get under way and proceed on our passage. Accordingly, we hove our anchor up at half past one o'clock on Sunday morning, the fourteenth of October. The wind blowing fresh, we took a reef in our main sail, and, as it was dark, one person was stationed in the bow of the boat, with a cutlass in his hand, that he might cut the rope in case we should see and could not avoid it.

"We had not run more than two hours when the one forward upon the look-out cried out to the man at the helm that the stakes were ahead, the boat going at so great a rate that the words were scarcely out of his mouth before we were foul of the rope, the man with the cutlass missing his blow. The tide was running so rapid that the boat upset and filled in an instant; seeing which, I sprang for the rope, and held on, while the boat was carried down with the tide.

Supposing it had sunk, having stone ballast in, I held on to the rope a few moments, when something coming across my hands broke them loose, and I was left on the water to shift as well as I could, the night being dark, and we at least ten miles from any land.

"It were impossible for me to describe my doleful apprehensions at this juncture. I cried, 'Lord, have mercy on me!' and saw no prospect but that this was all of earth to me. Hearing some of my companions hallooing, I joined in the general cry, hoping that some fishing boat might be near us. In this sad dilemma, I swam toward them, not supposing, at the same time, they had any better dependence than myself. But blessed be God! who in this trying time was near and ready to save by a providence all his own. It so happened, when the boat went down or upset, that the ballast tumbled out; therefore she floated, and, as I came up with the others, I found part of them holding on to the wreck, which kept them from sinking. But, alas! those gloomy waters that dismal night were already the grave of three of our number. These were Allen, Melvin, and the Frenchman, whom we never heard of more. Reflect upon this providential discrimination for thee, oh my soul, and bless God that thou wast not numbered with thy companions who met an untimely death.

"As soon as I had hold of the boat, I exercised myself immediately in securing some spars together to keep myself up, and in this condition fancied I was as safe as on land, comparatively speaking, and I thanked God for the signal interposition of his providence in saving me in so perilous a time. Had I been truly sensible of our critical situation, perhaps I should not have felt so easy, for we were now nearly eight miles from land, and the night very dark. Moreover, the wind beginning to blow quite hard, the swell rose so as to almost wash us from the boat. And, besides, the inhospitality of the Chinese is such that we had something to fear, rather than any thing to hope from them, in our difficult circumstances.

"While in this situation we felt the cold severely; the water was chilled, and we without clothing, for we had thrown the most part off, so that our condition was truly distressing. We drifted down with the tide and wind, without a glimmering of relief, until daylight, which was nearly three hours from the time we upset.

"As soon as it was fairly light, we discovered some fishing boats at anchor about two miles from us, and as the tide and wind drifted us directly toward them, our hopes revived, but only to sink again; for, the tide being nearly spent, we soon ceased to drift, and melancholy sat upon each countenance.

"We now joined our voices, in hopes that some of them might hear us; and, although we judged we were fairly within hearing, yet no one regarded. In this desperate and unfriended peril, one small ray of hope yet remained. The tide of flood being made, we saw several Chinese boats getting under way to beat up. After some time, one of them, standing across the bay, came pretty near us, and we made signs to them of our distress, but all in vain; they looked on and passed us by, like the priest and the Levite.

"But it pleased the Lord that we should not perish. In a short time after another boat came near, when, with our cries, and offering them a gold watch which one of the gentlemen had saved, besides one hundred dollars, they were prevailed upon to take pity on us and carry us to Macao. These, indeed, seemed to have some feeling for the distressed, for they gave us some clothes to put on (we having been about four hours in the chill water, and the weather quite cool), and some boiled rice and cakes to eat. We got the boat bailed out, and saved the most of the sails and rigging, and took her in tow with us to Macao, where we arrived at five P.M. the same day.

"Methinks if I ever exercised gratitude toward the Supreme Being for any deliverance, I did at this time, and not without resolutions to live henceforth in a very different manner from what I had done. Yea, I thought now none should ever turn me from my serious purpose of serving God. We remained in Macao until the Saturday following, repairing and fitting our boat in order to return to Wampoa, where we arrived on the Tuesday evening following, to the joy of all on board.

"By the twenty-sixth of December, our ship being loaded and ready for sea, we unmoored and dropped down the river, in company with the ship Hunter, Captain Homestead, bound to New York. December 28th, passed Macao, discharged the pilot, and stood to sea, with a fine breeze and glad hearts. We had a fine run to North Island, in the Straits of Sunda, where homeward-bound ships frequently touch for wood and water. As soon as we had brought our ship to anchor and furled her sails, on the thirteenth of January, 1793, we hove the boats out, and went with them wooding and watering. On the same day the Hunter came to anchor here also.

"The natives here are much more savage than at Ango Point, insomuch that we found it necessary to go armed with muskets and cutlasses, in case we should be attacked by them. Tuesday, the fifteenth, we sailed from North Island, and on the seventeenth left the Straits of Sunda. We stood into the latitude of about ten degrees south, where, having a good trade wind, we shaped our course for the Cape of Good Hope.

"At this time my mind took a more serious turn than ever on the things which concern the soul; and now I resolved to make religion the principal concern of my life. We had a favorable time until we arrived at the Cape of Good Hope, which was on the eighth of March. Here we lay trafficking and repairing our rudder, which was in bad condition, until the twenty-first of the same month, when we sailed for the West Indies.

"April 27th, in latitude sixteen degrees and twenty minutes north, and longitude fifty-seven degrees west, we saw a sail standing toward us; and, being desirous to speak her, we took in our light sails and laid aback. She soon came up with us, and proved to be a small armed sloop. We hailed her from whence she came. The answer was, 'From a cruise, and bound on a cruise.' At the same time we observed her decks to be full of men, and saw that she was armed to the teeth.

"Surprised and alarmed at this, not knowing any thing of the war between France and England, some believed her to be a pirate. As she passed along under our lee and wore ship, we cleared our guns and loaded them well, getting them all on one side. But when they came up with us the second time, they were more mild in their language, and informed us there was war in Europe, and that they had letters of marque and reprisal, and were cruising for French ships. They examined our papers, and being in want of water, we supplied them with a cask, and parted, happy to find it no worse.

"Monday, the twenty-ninth, made the island of Guadaloupe, and on the thirtieth came to anchor in St. Eustatia Roads, the ship Washington lying here, which had sailed eleven days before us from Canton. We lay in St. Eustatia till the eleventh of May, and then sailed for New York, where we arrived after a pleasant passage of eleven days, much rejoiced to see my native land once more, especially when looking back and reflecting what various and giant dangers I had escaped. Country and friends seemed dearer to me than ever before; the wish of my heart was that I might never leave them more, and I envied those who were quietly settled ashore."

HAPPY the man, not doomed afar to roam,
In distant lands, beneath a foreign sky,
Who hath a humble and secluded home,
Bathed by the little brook that prattles by,
With trees begirt, and birds that warble nigh.
He, as he sitteth in his humble state,
Hath little cause for earth's poor gauds to sigh;
He needs not envy whom the world calls great,
Who live in splendid house, with men that on them wait.

Chapter III.

RELIGIOUS CONVICTIONS, PROVIDENCES, TRIALS, AND TRIUMPHS.

Man's spirit hath an upward look,
And robes itself with heavenly wings;
E'en when 'tis here compelled to brook
Confinement to terrestrial things.
Its eye is fastened on the skies;
Its wings for flight are opened wide;
Why doth it hesitate to rise?
And still upon the earth abide?

T. C. Upham.

We have now reached a period in this autobiography when the powers of the world to come seized the subject of it with a grasp that was never after lost, though sometimes relaxed, until himself passed into that dread world. We have seen the growing seriousness of mind and gratitude to God induced by danger and deliverance, and that ease did not at once recant vows made in pain. His first act, on getting once more among his friends at Newark, was to offer up public thanks in church to the Author and Preserver of his life for his great goodness in restoring him in safety to his relatives and native land, and his language was that he had now resolved to make it the business of his life to seek and do the will of that God who had preserved him when in imminent danger, and when all hope had fled.

It was not long, however, that he remained ashore, his services being soon called for as mate of a vessel to the West Indies. During his absence at this time, his vessel was twice overhauled by privateers, and a prize-master put on board, and property belonging to Frenchmen confiscated. The second time he lay sick of a fever incurred in the port to which they had been ordered. Scarcely had they landed the condemned cargo and hastily taken another and stood out to sea, when they were boarded by the privateer Fanny and Polly, Captain Donald, who, after examining their papers and the passengers' trunks, upon suspicion of still having French property on board, ordered them to Jamaica, putting a prize-master and crew on board, and taking part of the vessel's crew on board the privateer. The sick mate they permitted to remain on board the schooner by reason of his illness. "This," he says, "was a trying time to me. The fever ran high, and, the cabin being full of passengers, there was no place where I could be comfortable, and scarcely any one to give me a drink of water.

In this situation I remained until we arrived at Port Antonia, on the east end of Jamaica. The next day after our arrival I went on shore and sent for a physician, who at once administered medicine. I continued extremely low three or four days, insomuch that there was little hope of my recovery.

"At this time my thoughts were much engaged about the concerns of my soul. I viewed myself as a great sinner threatened with death, and without hope, except such as arose from an idea that my prayers and cries might prevail upon the Most High to have mercy upon me. This, however, did not give me peace. I read the Bible whenever I was able; I repented because I was afraid of punishment; I made solemn vows, if the Lord spared me, that I would live a better life; and, at the same time, the tempter was permitted to fill my mind with thoughts too bad to mention. But my life was to be prolonged, to show what was in my heart. In about a week's time, through the skillfulness of my physician and good nursing, it pleased God that I should once more recover so far as to be able to walk about. Nevertheless, I remained still feeble, and under apprehensions.

"On the nineteenth we were ordered round to Kingston to take our trial. I was put on board a small schooner, a prize to the same privateer, and which they were taking round to have her trial likewise, having the said privateer in company with us. The next morning after we sailed we saw a sail which was supposed to be a French privateer; accordingly, we made the best of our way back to Port Antonia. The privateer and our schooner, being ahead of us, fell in with her, and finding her to be an English vessel, therefore made the best of their way to Kingston. I remained at Port Antonia until the twenty-eighth, and an opportunity then offering for Kingston, I embraced it, and arrived at that port September 1st. The same evening, being taken with a relapse, I went on shore, where I remained extremely low five or six days, after which time the fever abated, and I recovered appetite and strength.

"In the mean time the schooner was discharged, and such part of the cargo as appeared to belong to the passengers was condemned, and we were permitted to take the rest on board and proceed home. By the nineteenth of September I had so far recovered as to be able to go on board again, and on the twenty-first we dropped down to Port Royal, leaving our passengers behind at their desire, and on the twenty-third we sailed for New York. The day before, however, I was taken with a second relapse; and now, being out of the reach of a physician and those necessaries requisite in such cases, I was greatly alarmed.

"Daily growing worse, and expecting a long passage, knowing we had to go through the Gulf of Florida, my spirits sank, and I had nearly given up all hopes of seeing my native land ever again. But, blessed be God! it was determined otherwise. I continued extremely low until we had nearly reached the coast, insomuch that sometimes the captain despaired of my life; but, on approaching the land, and getting the weather a little cool, my appetite came again, and I once more began to mend."

Narrowly escaping shipwreck, they reached port on the twenty-eighth of October. Throughout that fall and the ensuing winter, up to the spring of 1794, he was subject to relapses of fever, which entirely laid him by, and did much to *im*pair his constitution, but much also, in the discipline of God's wise providence, to *re*pair and renovate his soul. He found, as many have, like David, that it was good for him to be afflicted, that he might keep God's law. Ill health went far to soften and subdue him, and make him put a true estimate upon sublunary things. It was a necessary part of the treatment he was undergoing by an all-wise Physician for the restoring of health to his soul. We think we see evidence that its effect upon him was that always meant and often realized by such schooling.

> The heart that God breaks with affliction's stroke,
> Oft, like the flower when stricken by the storm,
> Rises from earth, more steadfastly to turn
> Itself to heaven, whither, as a guide,
> Kindly, though stern, AFFLICTION still is leading,
> Even to the home of endless joy and peace.
> There, on the borders of that better land,
> Shall Pain's sharp ministry forever cease.
> Then shall we bless Thee, safely landed there,
> And know above how good thy teachings were;
> Then feel thy keenest strokes to us in love were given,
> That hearts most crushed on earth shall most rejoice in heaven.

By June of 1794 the health of our mariner was so far restored that he was able to undertake a voyage to the island of Curaçoa as chief mate of the brig Iphigenia; and in August of the same year we find him in command of the brig William for the same island, on the passage to which he was boarded successively by Spanish, French, and English privateers, but suffered to proceed.

Early in 1795 he is at Kingston, Jamaica, where he was again exposed to the yellow fever, and lost by it his chief mate and one of his men, all being more or less sick. He describes in the following manner, from eye-witness, the funeral ceremonies performed by the blacks in the island of Jamaica: "As soon as any person is dead, the connexions and acquaintance gather around the corpse, and begin to sing and dance, and play upon the banjo and other kinds of music as simple. When evening comes on, they gather in greater numbers, insomuch that their noise may be heard a mile. They continue in this manner until daylight, when they depart every one to his house. In the afternoon they assemble again, bring the corpse out into the yard, and, if it is a person of distinction among them, the coffin is very neatly painted and costlily furnished. Then they commence dancing, singing, and playing upon their musical instruments again, which they continue until near evening. When the corpse is taken up to be carried to the place of interment, two or three of the most distinguished among them are ornamented with ribbons in their hats, and, carrying colors, follow the corpse. The rest—men, women, and children—bring up the rear, with singing, dancing, and music as before. Thus they proceed until the person is interred, when each one returns to his place. I have been informed they have an idea that the soul of the deceased returns to its native country

(Guinea), and that music, dancing, &c., renders the soul more happy until it reaches its home."

Saved again from a grave in the West Indies, and narrowly escaping shipwreck on the Double-headed-shot Keys, Captain Congar returns to New York, and is immediately put in command of the new ship Alexander Hamilton, bound to the port of Nantes, France. On this European passage his human sensibilities as a benevolent and careful captain were greatly affected by losing overboard one of his sailors from the main yard. The voyage was successful, and he proceeded from Nantes to the Downs and London, and thence to St. Ubes, Portugal, for a cargo of salt. Dismasted, on the way back to New York, in a furious squall, their course was delayed; and they fell out of provisions, but were providentially supplied by another vessel fallen in with.

Soon after arriving at New York, he entered the marriage state, in January, 1796, with Miss P. V. Riper, of Newark, being himself in the twenty-eighth year of his age. Almost immediately after he sailed for Ireland and St. Ubes, and on his return was at once off again to Liverpool, taking his employer and family as passengers. The fourth day out, his employer died, and soon after a friend who had accompanied him, leaving his widow to the sympathy and care of Captain Congar, who himself fell ill with the same distemper that had carried off his passengers. He gratefully notices the sovereign mercy of God in his recovery, and in an opportunity afforded him in a succeeding voyage to save the crew of a leaky ship, at a great risk to his own.

Through perils in port and sea, by privateersmen and men-of-war, from terrific gales and prospect of foundering in a leaky ship, which he with difficulty kept his men from abandoning, we track his course through the pages of his journal up to 1798. It is always the course of a humane, upright, liberal, and conscientious American sea captain, yet without the peace of God, which passeth all understanding, keeping his heart and mind in Christ Jesus, and, consequently, not happy. On the ninth of May, 1798, he enters that his mind had been considerably exercised upon religion on the late passage to Madeira, in the ship Ceres.

"Having with me Hopkins's System of Divinity, I read it with great attention, my mind being particularly affected with that part which treats of the sins of all mankind being made manifest or revealed at the judgment. Knowing my sins to be of a crimson dye, I trembled at the thought of having them made known to the world; and, as I had often done in difficult circumstances before, so now I resolved to live more in the fear of God, and with a view to the judgment of the great day."

Severe trials now befell him in a course of disasters on ship-board, and the sickness of his wife, and his arrival at New York at the height of the prevalence of yellow fever in the summer of 1798, when seventy-two were falling victims to it in one day. "Death," he says, "seemed to brandish his scythe as though he were commissioned to cut down all. This passage in the Lamentations appeared to be verified in a particular manner: 'How doth the city sit solitary that was full of people!' Solitary indeed! I have passed through a whole street, and scarcely observed a soul moving.

"On one of these days of pestilence we cast off from the wharf. The wind being very light, our boy, who was about twelve years of age, was sent up to clear away the main top-gallant royal, but, on what account we never could learn, he had scarcely reached the top-gallant yard when he fell. Hearing something shock the deck, I cast my eyes around, and saw the boy lying on the companion way, flat on his face, and motionless. We took him up, supposing him to be dead, but he soon began to cry. We then rubbed him all over with camphor and spirits, and put him in a warm bed, and in less than a week he was able to walk considerably, and in a week more returned to his duty again. Had I not been eye-witness to these facts, I could not have believed it possible for any person to have survived such a fall."

This was the first of a train of difficulties that ran through this voyage. The first day out for Liverpool, yellow fever appeared on board, to their great dismay. Another of their most able-bodied seamen was thrown off duty by a severe fall, and fatal shipwreck was barely avoided on Sable Island. On the return, the journal says, "I believe it will not be far from the truth if I say we lay to almost every other day all the month of January; and about ten days before we arrived, as we were hove to, a heavy sea came on board, which knocked the long boat out of the chocks, washed away the booby-hatch, a great quantity of water going down in the steerage, stove in the quarter-boards, washed the binnacle overboard, and set us all afloat in the cabin. This happened while we were at supper, so that it made a clean sweep of every thing on the table. Fortunately, there was but one man on deck, and he had notice of it time enough to secure himself.

"February 22d, 1799, we made Sandy Hook, but it coming on to blow very hard from the northwest, we were under the necessity of letting go our anchors to prevent being blown off, though we were twelve miles from the land, and, consequently, pretty rough swell. Our anchors had not been down more than an hour when the small bower cable parted, and the other being insufficient to hold her, she continued to drag all night, so that in the morning we could scarcely see the Highlands of Neversink.

"The sea having broke over us fore and aft in the night, which froze instantly, our vessel appeared one solid body of ice from the stem to stern-post. At eleven o'clock next day, the weather moderating, we went to work clearing the ice off the decks, and hove up the anchor, but, to our mortification, there was little more than the stock left. The wind being from the westward, we could not get up to the Hook until the twenty-fourth. This night the cold was terrible; we could not come to anchor, for we had none, therefore were obliged to carry sail all night, in order to keep in with the land, and we barely escaped freezing. Next day we fortunately reached the city, through very much ice running in the channel. Thus ended a voyage begun with trouble and finished with hardships."

These extreme hardships had well-nigh driven Captain Congar from the sea. But, like the innately industrious every where, he found it harder to bear a want of employment than to brave the battle and the breeze; and, after four months of tedious shore life, we find him in an armed merchant ship, sailing in company with a fleet of others to the West Indies, for protection against pirates and privateers. In this voyage, only six of the forty that made up the complement of his ship, besides himself, escaped the West India fever; and eight of the number they buried on the island of St. Domingo.

The nineteenth century opened with a voyage to Bristol, England, in command of the ship Penelope; and it is at the close of this that we find the first satisfactory indications of the life of nature slain, and the life of God beginning in the soul of the mariner whose experience we trace. In another chapter we will pursue and develop those indications.

When I review my ways,
I dread impending doom;

But sure, a friendly whisper says,
  "Flee from the wrath to come."
I see, or think I see,
  A GLIMMERING FROM AFAR;
A beam of day that shines for me,
  To save me from despair.
Forerunner of the sun,
  It marks the pilgrim's way;
I'll gaze upon it while I run,
  And watch the rising day.

Chapter IV.

RELIGIOUS EXPERIENCE, PROFESSION, TEMPTATIONS, AND ESCAPE.

When I, in my distress, my anchor Hope can cast
Within the promises, it holds my vessel fast:
Safely she then at anchor rides,
Mid stormy blasts and swelling tides.

If a dead calm ensues, and Heaven no breezes give,
The oar of prayer I use, I tug, and toil, and strive:
Through storms and calms for many a day,
I make but very little way.

But when a heavenly breeze springs up and fills my sail,
My vessel goes with ease before the pleasant gale;
It runs as much an hour, or more,
As in a month or two before.

The Heavenly Mariner.

We are now entering the most remarkable period in Captain Congar's history—the period within which he solemnly consecrated himself to the service of his Maker, and entered into covenant relations with the visible church. In the month of June, 1800, he makes this entry in his journal: "Perhaps there have been few instances of a life spent like mine. Those religious impressions made on my mind, through the unwearied instruction and solicitude of a tender parent, could not easily be erased; so that, although convictions have been stifled and serious reflection banished at times when I have given myself up to abandoned wickedness, yet, when some afflictive providence has befallen me, or some threatening of God's wrath has been ready, as it were, to be executed on me, then I have thought upon my ways; so that by turns I have been the subject of great convictions, and then, again, would fall into the most abandoned licentiousness and profaneness.

"The difficulties experienced on the outward-bound passage of the last voyage seemed once more to rouse me up, and compel me, like the affrighted mariners of Tarshish, to call upon my God. Methought I took greater delight in reading the Scriptures than ever I had done before, many passages of which seemed to strike my mind with great force, and I wondered that I should have misimproved so great a boon as the Bible so long. I now once more formed resolutions to amend my ways, and not only lead a moral life, but, *through the assistance of God's grace, to become a Christian.* I felt, in a measure, my own weakness, and endeavored to look for strength from above; and when I arrived in Bristol, I attended public worship more constantly than had usually been the case before.

In the course of this voyage I often reflected upon the propriety of performing family worship when at home, and frequently resolved to make the attempt if I should be spared to return. But, alas! here I failed again. Surely I did not see the worthiness in Jehovah to be adored by all his intelligent creatures, or I would not have withheld the praises due unto his name.

"Nevertheless, before I went to sea again, I acquainted my wife that it was my wish to join in prayer with her morning and evening, which she acquiesced in, and for the first time I made the attempt. Soon after we sailed on another voyage to Bristol, through the course of which my mind was generally exercised, more or less, on the importance of religion, and particularly on the subject of family worship at home, which practice, through divine assistance, I was enabled to pursue when restored to them again. How far I was sincere in my devotions the Searcher of hearts knows best, but I have reason to conclude it was more the force of education than a real desire to glorify God. Be this as it may, I certainly was very ignorant of the nature of true religion."

From this time we find him more and more sensitive to sin, and also to the goodness of God, in his deliverance from a certain imminent danger. But he was plunging deep into the warfare described in the seventh chapter of Romans; and his experience now was that narrated with so much simplicity in the old "Dialogue between a Believer and his Soul."

Oh! I sink beneath the load of my nature's evil;
Full of enmity to God, captived by the devil:
Restless as the troubled seas; feeble, faint, and fearful;
Plagued with every sore disease, how can I be cheerful?

"Think on what thy Savior bore in the gloomy garden,
Sweating blood at every pore, to procure thy pardon:
See him stretch'd upon the wood, bleeding, grieving, crying;
Suffering all the wrath of God, groaning, gasping, dying."

This by faith I sometimes view, and those views relieve me;
But my sins return anew; these are they that grieve me.
Oh! I'm leprous, filthy, foul—quite throughout infected:
Have not I, if any soul, cause to be dejected?

"Pore not on thyself too long, lest it sink thee lower;
Look to Jesus, kind as strong, mercy join'd with power.
Every work that thou must do, will thy gracious Savior
For thee work, and *in* thee too, of his special favor."

Jesus' precious blood once spilt, I depend on solely,
To relieve and clear my guilt, but I would be holy.
"He that bought thee on the cross can control thy nature,
Fully purge away thy dross, make thee a new creature."

That he can I nothing doubt, be it but his pleasure.
"Though it be not done throughout, may it not in measure?"
When that measure, far from great, still shall seem decreasing—
"Faint not then, but pray and wait, never, never ceasing."

While in the experience of this conflict, Captain Congar's ship was again ordered to Ireland with a cargo of flaxseed, one of his owners being on board as a passenger. On their arrival they found that great numbers of the inhabitants were about leaving their native soil for the United States, and that some ships were already preparing to receive them. The prospect of gain, therefore, induced the owner to put up the newly-arrived American ship for passengers. As soon as the cargo was discharged, says the journal, we went to work putting up berths and building houses on deck for them. In the mean time, I was employed engaging them and receiving passage-money, which was at the rate of four guineas and a half for every full passenger.

"About the middle of April, having about three hundred engaged in all, including men, women, and children, we began to receive them on board. But such was the rage of this people for going to America, about eighty more made their appearance, so that at last I was much at a loss where to put them, and even then others came and begged for a passage, and would hardly take no for an answer. When they were all on board, our ship presented a little town, for we had no less than six houses on the quarter-deck that would hold about six or eight, and two on the main deck, each of which held eighteen; and, besides, we built a shed over the long-boat, where six or eight more took up their residence. Thus we set sail the twenty-eighth day of April, and on the second of May took our departure from Cape Clear. By this time many of them were very sea-sick, and would gladly have been on the turf again. But, alas! many of them were never to see it more.

"Unhappily for us, we had not been at sea many days before some of them were taken sick with a fever, and some with the dysentery, and though not many of them died while we were at sea, to such a degree had these disorders increased among them, that not less than eighty were sick when we arrived, several of whom lived but a short time after. Among the rest, I had a touch of the fever a few days before we made the land, but was so far recovered as to be able to attend to business when we got into port. Providentially, we had a favorable passage, or it would most likely have gone very ill with us indeed. We came to anchor at Staten Island in forty-two days, having buried at sea six adults and seventeen children; and, from what I could learn, about one hundred in all died before they left the quarantine ground.

One successful voyage after this to Madeira, and the sea life of Captain Congar is suspended for a few years, during which he assayed the business of a dry goods merchant at Newark. About this time we find the following entry: "Since my arrival from Madeira, my mind has been more engaged about religion than usual, which some of my friends observing, hinted to me, one evening, as we were walking to church, that the present would be a favorable opportunity of offering myself as a member, inasmuch as the Session were about to meet shortly for the purpose of examining such as came forward to join. This hint started me like one awaked out of sleep, and before I could make an answer, drew the conclusion that I was not fit; for, though I had thought some time past of offering myself as one desirous to join the Church, yet I had not brought the time so near. From this forward my thoughts have been more engaged about my situation, and have besought the Lord more earnestly that he would direct me to do that which should be most for his glory.

"When searching more attentively into my own heart, I found it exceeding hard and vile. Some persons, I found, could melt into tears when the idea of a crucified Savior was held up to view, and in my youthful days methinks I have felt something like this too, moving my passions when this subject has been preached. But now it was quite otherwise; my heart seemed harder than adamant, and sometimes I was tempted to conclude the Lord had left me to a state of impenitency and hardness of heart; and that, although there never appeared a more seasonable time to embrace religion, now I could not find it in my mind to do it, for my external performances did not satisfy me. I had done all that was required. I now cast myself upon the mercy of a gracious God, imploring his forgiveness, and that he would soften my hard heart, and lead me to sincere repentance and faith in Christ; and to my exceeding great comfort, surely the Lord was pleased to hear my request. Early on Sunday morning, the third of January, 1802, my mind was more than usually impressed with the importance of having an interest in the Redeemer's blood; and, feeling my helpless condition, I was led to seek God with my whole soul, that he would pardon my many transgressions, and heal a polluted mind, and teach me the way of life. Such were my exercises, that I rose to prayer before day, and then went down stairs to make a fire. While employed in this office, I began to sing,

"'Come hither, all ye weary souls.'

"At this time my soul seemed overcome with a sense of my great unworthiness, and of the adorable perfections of Jehovah. These wrought upon my mind so that I burst into tears. I again went on my knees, imploring the Divine direction that I might not be deceived, and that I might be preserved from offending God any more, desiring these impressions might be lasting. This was a pleasant Sabbath to me. If I be not deceived, I could truly say, One day in the courts of the Lord are better than a thousand elsewhere. My mind seemed to soar above the things of time and sense, and held converse with Heaven.

"I now formed resolutions to forsake every sin and follow God's commands. My mind has been composed, by turns, concerning my spiritual state, and by turns I have felt hardened, and sometimes indifferent, and at other times see so much vileness in myself that I can not help forming a conclusion that I am yet in the gall of bitterness and bond of iniquity; and then, like St. Paul, I find a law in my members warring against the law in my mind, and bringing me into captivity to the law of sin which is in my members.

"This evening, being at a conference meeting, I was called upon to pray, which, for the first time in public, I attempted, according to the best of my ability, but not without a sense of my great unworthiness and insufficiency. Shortly after, I lost sight, more or less, of that glorious character which had but a little before filled my mind with delight, so that when I attended meeting the Thursday following, I found very little comfort, and rather felt, as it were, condemned, and without hope. I was full of fear lest my ingratitude had provoked a just God to cast me off. These struggles in my mind broke me of my rest. The next day it pleased a merciful and all-wise Sovereign to give me such views of himself, that I felt willing to be in his hands, esteeming myself unworthy of the least mercy, and earnestly entreating that I might not be left to unbelief and hardness of heart, and that I might be enabled to lead such a life before him as would be acceptable through Jesus, the dear Redeemer.

"From this time onward till Wednesday, the twenty-seventh of January, 1802, I frequently had views of myself as a great sinner for neglecting so many precious calls and warnings, and misimproving so much precious time. At other times the character of God through Jesus Christ appeared so desirable, that my soul chose this God for my portion and hope, and methinks I find a greater pleasure in approaching the throne of grace than I have usually experienced. At this time I called to see one of the elders, to whom I related my exercises, and who told me he thought it would be proper for me to come forward on the next occasion and make a public profession of religion.

"Although my mind had been much exercised on this matter of late, yet I was not fully resolved what to do. I did not seem to fear the revilings of men so much as my own insincerity. Though it appeared the duty of every intelligent creature to love God with all his mind and strength, and the plan of salvation by Jesus Christ seemed reasonable, and fit, and worthy to be embraced by every son of Adam, yet I felt a great backwardness lest I should be deceiving myself and act the part of a hypocrite. Two days from this time I called to see Doctor M'Whorter, to whom I related my experience, and who seemed satisfied with the account I gave of myself. On Friday, the eleventh of February, in company with five or six others, I met the Session of the Newark Presbyterian Church, who heard our different relations, and we were dismissed. The Sunday following one of the elders called to inform me that, if it were my wish, I should be propounded the same day, it appearing proper to them that the others should wait till next opportunity. This Sabbath, if I be not deceived, I experienced some tokens of the Divine favor which strengthened me greatly in the cause I had embraced. But oh! the warfare within! How must we fight if we would come off conquerors!

"Sunday, February 28th, I was taken into the Church according to the customary regulations of the same, and methought the Lord appeared very gracious in strengthening and supporting me in so solemn a transaction; and I trust I felt rejoiced that I had been granted this opportunity of acknowledging my Lord and my Redeemer in this public manner. The Sabbath following, the sacrament was administered, and though I did not experience the Divine presence as some have done on these occasions, yet it was a profitable season. The wonderful condescension of Jehovah seemed very great in thus dealing with his sinful creatures.

"And now it was reasonable to expect that I should be more engaged to serve my Lord and Master than heretofore; but, alas! my foolish heart soon began to wander from my God, and a sort of lethargy or spiritual deadness seemed to accompany all my acts of devotion, insomuch that I could not avoid drawing unfavorable conclusions respecting myself. My heart seemed hard and my mind deeply blinded; but I was not suffered to remain in this state long without a chastising. Sabbath, March 14th, the Rev. Mr. Kollock preached in Newark from these words of our Savior to Peter, 'Lovest thou me?' While the preacher was setting forth the character of those who loved Christ in sincerity, my mind was deeply affected, and I feared very much I never had experienced what it was to love God and Christ with pure and holy motives; and, if so, I was yet in my sins, and without hope.

"These thoughts overpowered me to that degree that my nerves became exceedingly agitated and weak, so that it was with great difficulty I supported myself from falling.

"The only comfort that I could derive from past experiences was founded on my affection for the people of God. Finding myself quite feeble, and my mind deeply exercised, I did not go to church in the after part of the day, but implored the Divine presence and aid that I might not be left to perish in my sins, and that I might be enabled to love Christ Jesus with right views and motives, and be more engaged in following his commands. Doubts and fears, with some faint rays of hope, prevailed by turns, and sometimes the adversary seemed to almost get the advantage. But, blessed be the Father of mercies! about the first of June he was pleased to manifest himself to me (if I be not deceived) as lovely in all his character and government, and I rejoiced to have found him once more whom my soul loveth.

"Saturday evening, June 18th, being at a conference meeting, methinks I was greatly affected with the situation of a guilty world, and my heart's desire seemed to be that God would more abundantly pour out his Spirit, that careless sinners might be awakened, and see their need of a Savior, and that religion might increase and prevail over vice and infidelity. The day following, the sacrament of the Lord's Supper was administered, and there were thirty and one new members admitted to the communion. The scene was delightful to the friends of religion, and, if not deceived, my soul rejoiced in the event. Methought how lovely is this place. 'I had rather be a door-keeper in the house of my God, than to dwell in the tents of wickedness.'

"My prayer is, that I may have a humbling sense of my own unworthiness, and that I may live to the praise of my God and Redeemer all the days of my appointed time. Through the grace of God I am resolved to strive to this end. But, alas! what reason have I to lament my inconsistency. Not more than one fortnight had passed around when I began to fall into a lukewarmness, and a sort of spiritual sloth seemed to hang about every thing I engaged in. This dullness was followed by a disrelish for religious duties, and a sort of dread at meeting any of the principal members of the Church. On this account, or lest I should be called upon to pray or converse, I frequently neglected attending the evening societies; and with trembling I entered the courts of the Lord, for fear something might be spoken that would put me into confusion. And so far was I from exercising a spirit of meekness and forbearance, that, manifesting an unchristian temper one day, I was reproached with these words, 'Ah! where is all your boasted religion now?' Instead of being humbled under a sense of the dishonor I had brought upon the cause of Christ, I was highly offended at the person who made the expression. Forgive, O my God! what I thus confess with shame and confusion of face."

Hid by the clouds from sight, no sun did now appear,
Nor could I in the night behold the moon or star:

Twas then for days and weeks, or more,
I could not see the sky or shore.

The old elementary leaven of a certain natural instability of character now breaking out in Captain Congar, along with this departure from his first love, and merchandising having become tiresome as well as unprofitable, he sold the goods that remained on hand, and with the proceeds thereof embarked on a sort of trading expedition to Charleston, New Providence, and the Bahamas. In this he had but indifferent success, and returned safely, though ill at ease in his mind, to New York. And here he enters in his journal, "Now did it become me to have embraced the first opportunity of meeting with my friends in Newark, and offering up public thanksgiving to my Almighty preserver, who had blessed me with a great share of health, and restored me to my native country once more. Had my heart been right, I should have rejoiced that God was pleased to favor me with such an opportunity to declare his goodness, and his wonderful works to the children of men. But, alas! my conscience testified against me that I had departed from God; and on this account I felt such a backwardness of appearing among my Christian friends, that I took care not to be there on the Sabbath day, but went to church in New York, and experienced very little satisfaction or comfort therein.

"Thus about a month elapsed, when a circumstance happened that brought strong conviction to my mind that God was now about to chastise me for backsliding. As I was sitting at the breakfast table on the ninth of May, one of the company related a story which in some measure touched hard upon myself. I was immediately seized with a kind of tremor, and had to hurry from the table in confusion, endeavoring at the same time to conceal it as much as possible. From this time, let me go where I would, or in what company, I felt guilty, and my sins stared me in the face, so that I found no rest. Sometimes I resolved to flee away where nobody knew me, and at other times I despaired of finding peace on earth, and was tempted to drown myself. Thus was I harassed, continually beset with temptations and fears, till, on Saturday, May 21st, I went over to Newark, hoping I might find some relief to my mind ; but ah ! my sins followed me close. God had not done chastising me yet for departing from him.

"My wife and friends could not conceive what ailed me, neither was I able fully to convince them. I now began to give up all my hopes, and was bordering on despair. At this time I was strongly tempted to starve myself, from an apprehension that all these troubles were sent upon me for an over-fondness of indulging my appetite, and, dreading every thing here, I sometimes wished to die.

"Sunday being come, I knew it was my duty to go to church, but I was filled with such confusion and dread of appearing among my friends, or any body who knew me, that I had not resolution. Oh, the horrors of a guilty conscience! Though a return to God, by a deep and hearty repentance, was the only rational way I could hope for any comfort, yet I was so far from this, that I seemed determined on obstinacy and rebellion. I could not endure to see any of my acquaintance even at home, and I shunned the society of every body. My distress, indeed, compelled me to call on Rev. Mr. G., one of our ministers, and upon some of the elders, to whom I made known my difficulties. They all seemed to feel for me, and exhorted me to trust in God, through Christ; and told me it was no uncommon thing for the people of God to be exercised in this way more or less.

"I now began to consider myself as a vile hypocrite, and looked upon it as only adding sin to my guilt to pray in my family, or perform those external duties incumbent on professors of religion, and, for one time, I neglected prayer with this view. It is not easy to describe my feelings at this time. Astonishment took hold of me, and I was ready to cry out with the Psalmist, 'My confusion is continually before me, and the shame of my face hath covered me.' It often appeared as though my distress was, in a measure, such as the damned will experience, so far as it consists in a sense of their sins being known to the world; for it seemed as though every body knew all my crimes, and judged me.

"Thus I spent another week in this melancholy, dejected manner, and, Saturday evening being come, I summoned up resolution enough to attend society; but, looking upon myself as an outcast, and having forfeited all the blessings of social worship, I returned as I went, without consolation. Sabbath following I found myself still in the same difficulty as before, and could not form resolution to go to church, though being earnestly entreated by my wife for that purpose. In the evening, however, I attended a society, but without any relief to my troubled mind. Some of my friends told me that these things did not shake their hope for me as being a Christian. But, for my part, I could see every thing else in myself but the character of such a one.

" Though I had little heart to pray, or desire others to pray for me, yet now I could not think of giving it wholly up. Ingratitude seemed a monstrous sin in me. Tuesday, thirty-first of May, and the day following, I felt myself somewhat composed, and desired this trial might be sanctified to me: could read the Scriptures with some degree of pleasure, and endeavored to form resolutions, through Divine assistance, to seek the will of God, though he should still see fit to hide his face from me: striving to place my dependence on the merits of Christ alone for hope of acceptance, and renouncing my own works, which seemed, indeed, but as poor filthy rags. Friday, June 3d, being preparatory lecture, I was enabled to attend public worship, but, alas! the coldness and hardness of my heart, and how insensible to the Divine character and perfections. Such a stupor had seized my soul, methinks I received little benefit from this opportunity. I did, indeed, form resolutions to prepare for the duties of the following Sabbath, and, the day being come, with fear and trembling I entered the courts of the Lord. At first I was greatly confused, and had nearly sunk down; but, endeavoring to look for support from above, I seemed to be strengthened, and remained tolerably composed the rest of service time, and joined once more with the people of God in commemorating the dying love of a Savior, though not without doubts and fears. And, in proportion as they have the ascendency, so the delight in the ordinance must be proportionably less.

"And now, my soul, what hast thou done? Thou hast once more engaged to be the Lord's; not living to thyself, but unto him that died to save such an unworthy sinner. What gratitude dost thou not owe to thy Creator and Redeemer! Thou didst seek death and destruction, and yet he has brought thee to his banqueting-house; see to it, then, that thou dost perform unto the Lord thine oaths. Oh Lord, help me to perform. But, alas! my goodness was like the morning cloud or early dew, that vanisheth away; my resolution failed me, and melancholy returned, so that the next Sabbath found me in as great dejection and distress as ever before. And now every ray of hope seemed to be departing from me, and I began to conclude that I need not look for any peace or comfort here, and that the only remedy would be to wander away from all society, and take up my abode in some solitary clime among the savages, or others as ignorant as they.

"These reflections pierced me to the heart and brought many a sorrowful tear from my eye. What, said I, must I part with wife and friends, and never more behold them on this side the grave! how can I bear the thought? Sometimes, indeed, this little hope seemed left, that perhaps traveling would be the means of relieving my mind, so that I might once more take a little comfort on earth.

"I now gave my wife to understand that I intended going up the North River, first to a brother's I had living near Albany. To this at length she very reluctantly consented, and packed up some things for me; and on the fourteenth of June I left Newark with heavy heart; for though I gave her only to understand that my object in leaving home was merely to relieve my mind, which was true in some measure, yet nevertheless, harboring an idea that I should never more enjoy my friends at home, or take comfort again in my native place, I had secretly determined never more to return.

"With this view, when I got to New York I sold all my nautical books and instruments, giving up every thought of going to sea more; and not knowing whither I should go or how I should get a maintenance, I thought it advisable to take all the money I could conveniently get hold of, in case of the worst. I arrived at Albany in three days, and went at once to my brother's, who, with his family, received me gladly. But, as I had anticipated before, my mind was far from being calm and quiet. Though relieved, in a measure, from that embarrassment which I found at home, yet I became very melancholy and dejected, apprehending the judgments of God would pursue me wherever I went.

"I did not acquaint my brother with my real motive in leaving Newark, but rather hinted that it was on account of my temporal difficulties, and from a determination to quit the sea, and that, if I should undertake some laborious occupation for a maintenance, being so near the sea as Newark, I should be the more likely to give it up again, and betake myself to my former profession, for which I had conceived a great distaste.

"Before I left home, the thought had struck my mind, that as my brother understood the cut-nail business, probably we might undertake it with some advantage to us both. And now it appeared the only thing I could engage in that would suit the state of my health, both of body and mind, and be the means of procuring a support. This thought I soon made known to my brother, who, although he said it would be a great mortification to see me engaged in so low a calling, yet, if it was my sincere wish, he had no objections to join me in the business, not doubting but that we might make it answer a tolerable purpose.

"I now called forth all the powers of body and mind, went to work early and late, and made rapid progress in the knowledge of this new art, so that in two or three weeks I could make as handsome a nail as others who had followed it a much longer time.

"Although I attended public worship constantly at Troy, and evening conferences where my brother lived, yet I was often, on these occasions, much confused and distressed, so that it frequently appeared to me I must fly again, and whither I knew not. These reflections wrung me to the very heart, and I endeavored to look up to God that he would pass by my many transgressions, and bring about means that I might be restored to my family and friends again, but fearing this was never to be my lot more."

I thought the brute creation were better off than me;
I spent my days in anguish, no pleasure could I see:

Through deep distress and sorrow my Savior led me on,
Then show'd his love unto me when all my hope was gone.

While suffering these sore temptations, and in this strangely unnatural state both of body and mind, Captain Congar endeavored to persuade his wife to dispose of their property at Newark, and come and take up her abode with him. She at once yielded to his desire that she would visit him, but her entreaties, and a better judgment, perhaps, in this matter, persuaded him to abandon a line of life for which he was all unfit, and to consent to return to Newark. But apprehensive, he says, that I should labor under the same difficulties when I got among my friends that I had experienced before, I obtained a promise from my wife that, should this be the case, she would accompany me somewhere to a more southerly climate. But, alas for him,

In vain the unhappy rover flies,
In hopes of finding happier skies;
In vain he changes clime and air,
For still unhappy self is there.

"The unhappy state of my mind led me to grasp at any thing that would promise relief. In the fore part of August I made my appearance in Newark, but very little better composed than when I left it last, and, if possible, more regardless of the ties of friendship and every social relation. I seemed now to myself to have lost all good-will and affection for every one here, even those to whom I had been strongly attached. I took no delight in religion nor society, and thus passed my time like some solitary being who is displeased with himself and all around him; who, though surrounded with the good things of life, enjoys nothing, and is only happy when sleep drowns the anxiety of a disturbed mind.

"In this condition the soul finds little peace; sometimes under the most dreadful apprehensions about futurity, and then only concerned for the present; often wishing for death, yet afraid to die. At one time I acknowledged the justness of my punishment, and at other times was tempted to fret and complain because I was thus dealt with, continually resolving and unresolving, a compound medley of unruly passions. For the first three or four days after my return I was pretty generally fixed on setting off again, dreading the Sabbath should come, being apprehensive I should not be composed enough to go to church; and so it happened, for I could not form resolution to make the attempt. I still continued sad and solitary, and though I felt that help must come from God alone, yet had I very little heart to pray. The denunciation in the prophet Isaiah seemed very applicable to my case: 'And the pride of Israel testifieth to his face; and they do not return to the Lord their God, nor seek him for all this. Ephraim also is like a silly dove without heart; they call to Egypt, they go to Assyria. When they shall go, I will spread my net upon them; I will bring them down as the fowls of heaven; I will chastise them, as their congregation hath heard. Wo unto them, for they have fled from me; destruction unto them, because they have transgressed against me; though I have redeemed them, yet they have spoken lies against me. And they have not cried unto me with their heart when they howled upon themselves. Though I have bound and strengthened their arms, yet do they imagine mischief against me. They return, but not to the Most High; they are like a deceitful bow.'

"Toward the latter part of the week the Lord was pleased to remove his stroke from me in some measure; I began to feel somewhat cheerful, and could go among my friends without experiencing such confusion. Nevertheless, it remained a matter of doubt with me whether I should feel composed enough to attend public worship the ensuing Sabbath.

"On Saturday evening, the thirteenth of August, my brother's wife had been to pay us a visit, and, with true Christian charity, reproved me pretty sharply for the neglect of so important a duty. I did not feel in the least offended at her for this, but soon began to make up my mind to go to church next day, endeavoring to look to the Lord for assistance. Blessed be his name, I was enabled to wait upon him in his house, and my mind was generally composed through the day; I esteemed this an unmerited favor, and desired to be truly thankful. Finding a degree of tranquillity restored to my mind, my thoughts of leaving home again, on this occasion, have vanished, and, through the whole week, have been more composed than has been the case for some time. But I still experience a great dullness in religious duties, and little pleasure in the company of Christians.

"Saturday evening, the twentieth of August, I attended a conference meeting, rejoicing once more that I had an opportunity of joining with the people of God in religious exercises, and grateful for this instance of Divine compassion and forbearance, resolving now to return to him from whom I had deeply revolted. Sabbath following I went to the house of God with considerable satisfaction, and pretty well composed, but without those consolations of the Holy Spirit which are so reviving to a soul in distress. Still I endeavor to wait upon God and hope in his word, confessing my unworthiness to receive any mercy. The next Friday a lecture was delivered, preparatory to the sacrament, from these words: 'Looking diligently, lest any man fail of the grace of God.'

"The Sabbath following I joined once more with the people of God in commemorating the dying love of a Savior. One great end brought to view by this ordinance seemed to be the necessity of living on Christ by faith, as the body is nourished by bread and wine. From this time my mind became more composed, and I no longer thought of leaving Newark again, as on a late occasion, but endeavored to commend myself to the Lord, and wait his will with respect to temporal as well as spiritual concerns."

And now the cloud is lifted, and light is once more breaking upon the tried and tempted Christian mariner, faith and submission having been inwrought into his soul by the discipline of a gracious Providence. This ever is the way of God with the soul of man. He bends the human will into sweet acquiescence with HIS own will by trials and mortifications, and, that secured, then there can be permanent joy and peace.

> The path of sorrow, and that path alone,
> Leads to the land where sorrow is unknown.

Sorrowing and troubled reader, whosoe'er thou art, cast down, perhaps, and almost despairing, only sweetly yield thy will to God's, and then thou shalt cheer up and take courage.

In the day of visitation,
  When the clouds have o'er thee passed,
And thou thinkest that salvation
  May not bless thee at the last;
In the hour of doubts and fearing,
  When the Savior seems afar,
And thy spirit, without cheering,
  Is the night without a star—
Know that it is all to try thee,
  And that Jesus loves thee still;
Nor will ever He deny thee,
  If thou walkest IN HIS WILL.

He hath set the great example,
  Follow on, as he hath trod;
Doubts and sin beneath thee trample,
  Live, and act, and hope in God.
Then, though light or dark attend thee,
  In the end 'twill be the same;
If the Savior doth befriend thee,
  Thou shalt ne'er be put to shame.

Chapter V.

NAVIGATING FOR ETERNITY. THE LIGHTS AND SHADOWS OF THE CHRISTIAN LIFE.

Thou Star of the Christian! thou Guide of the lost!
  Oh, withhold not the beams that can lead and can gladden
Frail man on the ocean of life when he's toss'd;
  When the billows run high, and the wild tempests madden.
Blest Savior! once more be the light of my soul;
  And, amid all the dangers and griefs that oppress me,
This heart shall submit to thy faultless control,
  The song of these lips shall unceasingly bless thee.

T. C. Upham.

Upon the mountain wave we mount again with our mariner, whom a call, deemed by him providential, induces to make his home once more on the deep. Having command of the ship Enterprise, and taking with him his wife, he sailed for Cork, Ireland, on the twenty-eighth of August, 1803. The voyage seems to have been propitious, and its issue all that could be desired, his own health and spirits being better for engaging in an employment to which he had been trained, and his wife's health also improving. With a becoming piety, he took occasion of the first Sabbath after his return to offer up public thanksgiving to his gracious Preserver;

and, though he was not yet entirely free from those embarrassments of mind that had before so greatly afflicted him, he endeavored to look to the Most High for support and submission.

Early in 1804 he sailed again to Wilmington, North Carolina, and thence to Hull, England, where he notes with gratitude that he had frequent opportunities of public worship with "a sacred pleasure therein." An offering of thankfulness was duly paid in the Lord's house on his return, and we find him saying that "at this time the Lord was pleased to grant me those consolations of his blessed Spirit which are so reviving to an afflicted soul. Every time I met in public worship while at home, I enjoyed more or less of the comforts of religion, and could join with my brethren in society with considerable freedom and delight."

On a subsequent voyage, being again at Wilmington, on his way to Bristol, and without the company of his wife, he writes, "I experience the want of society much, and sometimes, alas! I feel very low-spirited; but God is still gracious. I enjoy a great share of health, and am not without the consolations of his Spirit, I would hope. True, it is desirable to have always the assurance of blessedness; but are we to look for this at all times? It is a mercy that such a sinner as I am is at this moment out of the regions of woe. May my spared life be spent for the glory of God.

"Near the coast of Europe, Sunday, January 27th, 1805. This day my soul is much cast down. I view myself as a great sinner. Oh, how vile is the human heart! it is deceitful above all things. How exceeding sinful does sin appear, and mine in a particular manner aggravated; but, though my sins appear like huge mountains over my head, ready to burst forth upon me, yet I would look to God in Christ for pardon and sanctification."

The grounding of his ship in trying to go over the Swash at the mouth of the Avon, made it necessary to put her into dock for repairs, and this delayed his return, but he sought and found comfort in the society and worship of God's people while in port. Finding, after getting out to sea, that one of his passengers was a minister, he solicited his services as preacher all the Sabbaths of the passage.

The following summer he made a very agreeable voyage to Madeira with his wife for a cargo of wine, in the course of which he had many occasions to note the Providence and mercy of God, which he duly remembered in public thanksgiving on his return. It was now, however, that the natural instability of character we have before remarked upon, joined, perhaps, with a diminution of bodily vigor as he advanced in life, set him upon thinking again to quit the sea; and these are his reasonings upon it:

"It is a life fraught with difficulty and care, anxiety and perplexity. We frequently experience much trouble with the crew, as was the case the last two voyages. We are greatly exposed to temptation; we are deprived of the principal sources of happiness in this life, society, and the opportunity of meeting with the people of God on Sabbath days; and those who have families, with whom they live in habits of mutual affection, striving which can be most kind and tender, and whose greatest pleasure is to make each other happy, must necessarily feel great anxiety at parting with them, and being absent so long a time without an opportunity of hearing from one another. At one time duty bid me go; at another time the same reason influenced me to stay; so that we were nearly ready for sea before my mind became settled which way to act. I made it my request, in all my supplications to the throne of grace, that I might be directed in this important matter; and I desire to be thankful that

God heard me, for my mind became calm and settled, and it appeared clearly my duty to engage again in this business; and seeing no other way opened whereby I might be useful in life, I became reconciled, and submitted to the pain of leaving my bosom friends, and, I may add, almost every thing that renders life pleasant, to seek my bread upon the great waters.

"And now I pray God that I may go in his name and in his strength to the work that is before me, that he would enable me to fulfill every duty incumbent on me in the sphere wherein I am placed; that he would grant me his blessing and presence, and restore me to my family and friends in his own good time, richly laden with experience of his goodness and loving-kindness.

"In setting out on this voyage, several discouraging circumstances took place, which were by no means calculated to compose the mind at a time like this. Monday, January 13th, 1806, we hauled the ship off into the river, that we might be in the more readiness to proceed with the first wind. The day following, a snow and hail storm came on from the northeast; wherefore we thought it advisable to haul the ship into the wharf again. It being extremely cold, with difficulty we got her secured before night, leaving two anchors off in the river. Wednesday, 15th, the wind was favorable, but, blowing a gale, this day we spent in getting our anchors on board again.

"Thursday the weather continued intolerably cold, insomuch that we found it difficult to loose the sails, that we might get them softened a little. The ice now began to make fast. Friday, the 17th, the weather moderated, and the wind continuing favorable, we set sail, and had a very good time down to the Hook, and getting to sea. In no instance that I recollect has my mind been more tranquil and composed at the time of leaving my native shores; but this desirable peace did not abide with me long ere I had to feel the want of that society I had left. Now I became dejected and disconsolate, and sometimes it seemed as though I should not be able to bear up under the load of melancholy.

"The fifth day after we sailed came on a tremendous gale of wind from the southeast, at which time our ship began to leak very badly, and the steward, being taken very ill of a pleurisy at the same time, I had to officiate myself in that capacity. Under all these discouragements, I endeavored to rest my hopes on the Rock of Ages; from God I sought relief, and with gratitude I would acknowledge I have found relief. January 28th, 29th, and 30th. The winds are adverse, yet my mind is quite composed, and I feel willing the Lord should do what seemeth him good, and, blessed be his name, if I am not deceived, I do enjoy religion even here.

"Saturday, the 8th day of February, we experienced a gale of wind from the westward, in the course of which we were struck by three very violent seas, which damaged our boat over the stern considerably, and even threatened the safety of us all. I arose, and called upon Him who holdeth the winds in his fists and the waters in the hollow of his hand, and the Lord was pleased to hear the request of a poor sinful creature. The violence of the winds and seas abated, and we were delivered from our fear.

"From this time we had a considerable spell of favorable winds, so that we made good progress on our way. One important end may be answered by this solitary life which I have upon the seas, which could not be attained so well in the midst of society: I now call to mind the sins of my whole life, and reflect upon them with repentance. I have an opportunity to search out the evil nature and consequences of sin; this leads me to self-abhorrence on account thereof, and to admire the wonderful forbearance of God in sparing so great a rebel. In general, my mind is tolerably well reconciled to my situation, except on Sabbath days. It is then that my soul looks to the land of inhabitants meeting together for social worship. But why should I complain? Have I improved the advantages of society, and the many opportunities I have been favored with, of hearing the Gospel preached? Alas! no. I feel unworthy of any of the comforts of life, and yet I daily experience many. I enjoy a great share of health, and have the continuation of my rational faculties, and still am preserved on the mighty deep. Methinks I never have had such affecting views of the evil of sin as I have had at sea, particularly in the course of the last voyage to Bristol, and also for a few days past. It seems wonderful there should be so much happiness in a world so full of it. This appears to be the procuring cause of all the evil we suffer in this life, or dread in that which is to come. I trust I feel grateful to the blessed Spirit for opening my eyes to see sin to be so exceeding sinful, and affording me any hope of salvation from it this day, eighteenth of February."

There are repeated instances in this part of

Captain Congar's autobiography of his resorting to the Bible when under apprehension of losing his ship by the dangers of the seas, and finding its promises to afford him sweet relief; so that he could say from his own personal habit as a Christian mariner,

The Bible is my chart; by it the seas I know;
I can not with it part, it rocks and sands doth show:
It is a chart and compass too,
Whose needle points forever true.

When through a strait I go, or near some coast am drove,
The plummet forth I throw, and thus my safety prove;
My conscience is the line which I
Fathom the depth of water by.

My vessel would be lost in spite of all my care,
But that the Holy Ghost himself vouchsafes to steer;
And I through all my voyages will
Depend upon my Steersman's skill.

Once, when winds used to become contrary, he bore it impatiently, and would grumble; but now he could cheerfully submit, and behold the faithfulness of God in all his dealings, and we hear him say, "In some good measure I find myself believing that God is infinitely wise and good in all that he does, and therefore worthy to be submitted to and confided in under all the vicissitudes of life. And besides, how many instances could I call to mind wherein I have been delivered from death in a manner miraculous; and I am now experiencing great health and innumerable mercies. Wherefore, oh my soul, be no more stiff-necked and rebellious, but rather seek to possess the temper of the prophet, who says, 'Though the fig-tree shall not blossom, neither shall fruit be in the vine; the labor of the olive shall fail, and the fields shall yield no meat; the flocks shall be cut off from the fold, and there shall be no herd in the stalls, yet I will rejoice in the Lord, and joy in the God of my salvation.' April 29th, the wind still remains unfavorable, but, if I am not deceived, I feel this day such a complacency in the Divine character, that I can rejoice in some good degree with the prophet above."

Sunday, May 17th, 1806, on the passage back to Wilmington, he writes, "My mind for some days past has been more deeply affected with my spiritual condition than usual. I ponder on my sins, I weigh my actions, I judge myself, and frequently doubt the sincerity of my profession. Although my sins have been of a crimson dye before I joined the Church, yet my greatest doubts arise from a view of tho inconsistency of my conduct and temper since that event took place. These reflections pierce my soul with bitter mourning and lamentations. Once methinks I walked in the light of God's countenance, could call the Savior mine, but now his face is hid, and I am troubled; I am bowed down; my sins have gone over mine head as a heavy burden; I am greatly oppressed. Sin, that dreadful enemy of the soul, hath caused all this."

Come, Holy Ghost, and blow
  A prosperous gale of grace;
Waft me from all below,
  To heaven, my destined place!
Then in full sail my port I'll find,
And leave the world and sin behind.

Rather more than a year from this date, after much experience of danger and deliverance in the course of two voyages to Liverpool, we find this entry on the twenty-sixth of June, 1807: "This day closes the thirty-ninth year of my age. Alas! I have to mourn much misspent time, many shortcomings, and little progress in the Divine life; and, notwithstanding so many imperfections, and so prone to go astray as I yet remain, the Lord has been gracious to me in a variety of instances through the year past. May my soul be filled by humble gratitude, and may I be enabled, by Divine assistance, to live henceforth through the rest of my days more becoming one who has professed to be a follower of the blessed Redeemer."

Saved by grace, I live to tell
  What the love of Christ has done
He redeem'd my soul from hell,
  Of a rebel made a son:
Oh, I tremble still to think
  How secure I lived in sin;
Sporting on destruction's brink,
  Yet preserved from falling in.
In a kind, propitious hour,
  To my heart the Savior spoke;
Touch'd me by his Spirit's power,
  And my dangerous slumber broke:
Then I saw and own'd my guilt;
  Soon my gracious Lord replied,
"Fear not, I my blood have spilt,
  'Twas for such as thee I died."

"Methinks it would be well for every person, if possible, to keep a sort of journal or memorandum of the most material occurrences in life. Though many, perhaps, would have nothing to notice that others would feel interested in, yet surely a history of one's own life ought to be of the most consequence to us above all others. We take great pains to obtain a knowledge of the lives and characters of others, and this may be well; but surely we ought to know something about ourselves, which can not well be done if we neglect to notice events as they pass. Thus, for instance, to-day I feel considerably composed and cheerful, and am enabled to rejoice in that good Hand which hath guided me through so many difficult scenes; and I do now purpose to live while I be spared more in the exercise of a gracious temper and disposition, under the various dispensations I may be called to pass through, and to be more engaged in the great concerns of eternity; but, behold, to-morrow's sun finds my sins continually swell before my eyes like huge mountains, and though I deeply lament for my transgressions, still I find my soul prone to wander from God. This gives me disquietness, oh wretched man that I am!

"July 10th. I am still oppressed by the weight of my sins; more and more do I seem convinced of the iniquity and deceitfulness of my heart. But, under these melancholy apprehensions, the Scriptures afford a ray of hope. Therein do we discover that God is merciful and gracious. He says to the humble and contrite, 'Though your sins be as scarlet, they shall be white as snow; though they be red like crimson, they shall be as wool.' Nevertheless, I am still in difficulty lest my repentance be only legal, and arise merely from a dread of the misery my sins have brought upon me. And, besides, the Scriptures declare that only he that believes in Christ shall be saved, and here also I want evidence. But the Scriptures inform us that Christ Jesus came into the world to save the chief of sinners, and such am I, and such as I need salvation most. Therefore there is room for hope that his grace may also be bestowed on me."

He lives to silence all my fears,
He lives to stop and wipe my tears;
He lives to calm my troubled heart,
He lives all blessings to impart.
He lives and grants me daily breath,
He lives, and I shall conquer death;
He lives my mansion to prepare,
He lives to bring me safely there.
He lives my kind, my heavenly friend,
He lives and loves me to the end;
He lives, and while he lives, I'll sing,
HE LIVES MY PROPHET, PRIEST, AND KING.

A month or two after this outpouring of a gracious soul, we find him again sitting apart like a dove, and mourning over his corruptions. "Every day methinks I behold more and more vileness in my heart, which, indeed, as the Scriptures express it, has been the cage of every unclean bird. Could I but trace out one single good action that had proceeded from a pure principle of love to God, I had some ground of hope; not that I should merit forgiveness for such good action, but only as an evidence there might be a small spark of grace in the heart, notwithstanding its dreadful corruption."

On his return from sea in the fall of 1807,

and offering up public thanksgiving, as his manner was, to Him who holdeth the winds in his fists and the waters in the hollow of his hands, he found a very extraordinary revival of religion had begun in Newark and vicinity, of which he thus takes notice: "At this time the inhabitants of my native town were much engaged in religion, and it appeared the Lord was about to do wondrous things among us. I had resolved to stay at home this winter, partly on account of the threatening difficulties from the belligerents, and partly because the voyage was intended to be a very long one, as before, and I found my constitution rather unable to bear so long the hardships of the sea.

"Now I had opportunity of meeting with the people of God almost every day or evening, and at times methinks I enjoy this favor. The first Sabbath in March, 1808, there were added to the Church ninety-seven persons, and the probability is there will be as many on the next sacramental occasion.

"The time for administering the sacrament beginning to draw near, and my mind having for a considerable time been very uneasy respecting my spiritual condition, I now have given myself to serious inquiry into this matter, and have resolved by Divine assistance to seek

God by fasting and prayer, that I may know whether I be in the faith or not; being persuaded that I never can be useful as a member of the Church while I remain so beset with doubts and fears.

"Sabbath, June 5th, the sacrament was administered. With thanksgiving I desire to mention the exceeding goodness of God to me this day. I trust I had some views of a Savior precious to my soul, and my doubts and fears are banished in a great degree. Oh! how wonderful is the faithfulness of our God. At this time my elder brother, who had been laboring under great difficulty of mind, and seemed bordering on despair, found relief, and was enabled to rejoice in the Savior once more.

"Sabbath, June 26th. This day methinks I have enjoyed a visit from my Savior. Oh! how kindly does he draw by the cords of love, and how pleasant was it to wait upon God in his sanctuary."

Beneath his cooling shade I sat,
To shield me from the burning heat;
Of heavenly fruit he spreads a feast,
To feed my eyes and please my taste.

Kindly he brought me to the place
Where stands the banquet of his grace.
He saw me faint, and o'er my head
The banner of his love he spread.

With living bread and generous wine
He cheers this sinking soul of mine;
And opening his whole heart to me,
He shows his thoughts how kind they be.

Oh! never let my Lord depart;
Lie down and rest upon my heart.
I charge my sins not once to move,
Nor stir, nor wake, nor grieve my love.

"Monday, June 27th, 1808. This day I have entered upon the forty-first year of my age. Alas! when I look back upon my life past, what do I survey but a scene of rebellion the greater part, and base ingratitude for unmerited favors. But as the stubborn and rebellious Jews were destroyed in the course of the forty years in the wilderness, so may all my corruptions be slain, and may I now engage, as it were anew, upon the service of my Creator and Redeemer. From this time onward until the first of December, I trust I was enabled to rejoice in God my Savior. I felt that all my salvation was of free grace. I can now take a sincere pleasure in public and private duties of worship, and in the society of Christians. If I be not deceived, I felt strong desires for the salvation of poor sinners, and I was enabled to see how God could be glorified, and to rejoice in it; and methinks I felt such confidence in his faithfulness that I could commit to him all my future destinies."

Having pursued thus far through the lights and shadows of the Christian life herein traced, we leave our navigator for the present in this happy estate, the race of his life just half run; praying that the peace of God which passeth all understanding may in like manner be the portion of every earnest mind that peruses these pages.

SAY not 'tis all a dreary way,
  With rocks beset, with briers growing,
Where never beams of sunlight stray,
  And ne'er a gentle stream is flowing.
Or, if it be that thou dost stray
  Through scenes so darksome, wild, and frightful,
Yet there is one who loves thee so,
  That he can make e'en this delightful.
Then drive away thy doubts and fears,
  Nor dread the ills that threat to hurt thee;
For Christ, that saw thee in thy tears,
  Hath said, He never will desert thee.

FOOTMAN in the heavenly race—
Fellow-sinner, saved by grace,
If thou hast indeed begun
In the heavenly way to run—
Many a cloud will gather o'er thee,
Many a trial lies before thee,
Many a wild along the way
Waits to tempt thy foot astray;
Many a hill, whose rugged road
Will not let thee bear thy load

(Save the inseparable cross),
Thou must climb, and leave thy dross.

But there waiteth at the end
Such a home and such a Friend,
Such a crown and such a throne,
Such a harp of heavenly tone,
Such companions, such employ,
Such a world of hallow'd joy!
And thou hast, along the way,
Many a promise for thy stay;
Strength and comfort from above,
Heavenly hope and heavenly love!
Footman, speed thy heavenward pace,
Trust in God, and win the race.

CHAPTER VI.

LABORS WITH HIMSELF AND LABORS IN BEHALF OF THE SABBATH FOR SEAMEN.

WE'RE often like the lonesome dove that mourns her absent mate,
From hill to hill, from vale to vale, her woes she doth relate:
But Canaan's land is just before, sweet spring is coming on;
A few more beating winds and rains, and winter will be gone.
Sometimes like mountains to the skies, black Jordan's billows roar,
And make us weary pilgrims fear we never shall get o'er:
But when, as from Mount Pisgah's top, we view the vernal plain,
To fright our souls may Jordan roar, and hell may rage in vain.

TIEBOUT'S *Hymns.*

THE web of human life is always party-colored: the tissue of the soul's history especially is made up of many threads, some black, some bright, and all closely interwoven with one another. The fabric of religious experience unrolled in the present chapter is of this description; for in the life of Captain Congar, as in that of most other men, the clouds followed sunshine, storm came after calm, and a day of brightness and joy was frequently succeeded by a night of gloom. Men's faults, according to the dramatist, would despair if they were not nursed by their virtues; and our virtues would grow proud if they were not whipped by our faults.

Early in the spring of 1809 we find him instituting a rigid self-examination, taking himself seriously to task, and sighing like Job, 'O that it were with me as in months that are passed, when the candle of the Lord shined upon me.' "We naturally love," says he, "pleasant gales and a smooth sea; but when the rough winds of adversity begin to blow, how soon do our spirits sink. Not long since I trust I could say with a good degree of sincerity, 'The Lord is my portion; what need I more!' I fondly hoped I should never again be exercised with doubts and fears; but ah! I have reason to fear that I looked too much to my own self, and forgot that, without Christ, I could do nothing. The state of my mind being so very different from what it was last summer, I have endeavored to draw a contrast between my exercises then and now. The Divine character, perfections, and government appeared to me then admirable and lovely, and every way worthy the chief regard of all intelligent creatures. Now these glories seem hid, or otherwise the mind is so exceeding dull and stupid that it takes very little satisfaction in meditating on them.

"Then I felt a sweet dependence upon the grace of God for all I needed both for time and eternity. Now the thoughts are employed much of my time in seeking to do something on the score of law, and frequently intent on quieting conscience. Then methinks I relied entirely on the atonement of the blessed Redeemer for all hope of pardon and acceptance with God, and cordially embraced him for my Savior and my portion. Now the excellences of the Redeemer are not seen but at a distance, and the soul is bent on seeking some good work, or falls into melancholy. Before, there was an inconceivable composure of mind, that was pleased at all times, and could look forward to a never-ending eternity even with delight. Now the mind knows but little of such feelings; but, on the other hand, there is considerable anxiety for my future state. Then was experienced a liberty of soul, a deliverance from the shackles of Satan, and freedom from the reigning power of sin. Now new temptations arise, the mind is filled with fears and doubts, difficulties increase, and I am in trouble, constantly harassed with vain and sinful thoughts. Then methinks I could approach the throne of grace with an humble boldness, and, though my desires were ardent for some particular mercies, especially the salvation of one who was dear to me, yet I felt a calm submission that could leave all in the hands of God and say, His will be done. Now the duty of prayer is, I am ashamed to say, burdensome; there is too often a want of liberty, the mind is much disturbed with wanderings, and there is very little sense of the great privilege granted to sinners in thus holding converse with the Most High. Then the society of Christians was pleasant and comfortable, and the affection they shared in my heart was strong and sincere, and much I enjoyed in their company. Now such seasons I realize not. I am sensible of very little fellowship with Christians, and there is frequently a disposition to shun their society; however, I can not say that I fully take pleasure in the society of those I deem destitute of religion. Then, if I be not deceived, I felt a benevolence and good-will toward my fellow-creatures, and strong desires for their salvation as connected with the glory of God; but at present a great indifference prevails with regard to both these objects. Ah! how little is to be enjoyed in the soul without religion in present exercise!"

A morbid melancholy now possessed him for a little season, and his mind preyed upon itself, owing mainly to a want of steady, satisfying employment while off the sea. But the severe self-scrutiny and sorrow for sin he underwent resulted in benefit to his Christian character, and to the establishment of his soul in grace. At length, on the twenty-fourth of April, 1809, we find this entry in his journal:

"An arrangement being fixed upon between the British minister and our government for the renewal of commerce, I have this day taken command of the ship Atlas, belonging to the house of W. Neilson & Son, in whose employ I had been before the embargo took place. I trust I entered upon this business with prayer to God that I might be enabled to seek his glory in all my pursuits, and be useful to my fellow-creatures in the sphere wherein I am placed. I feel, indeed, insufficient for the duties of my station, but I endeavor to look up to the Lord for direction and support. This ship being nearly loaded before I took charge of her, we had but little to do in order to get ready for sea.

"May the 11th we left New York, and on the 13th sailed from Sandy Hook with a fine breeze, which scarcely left us until we were at anchor in King Road, being thirty-three days from New York. We sailed again from Bristol on the eighth day of August, with a full freight for New York.

"On the 19th of October, after being seventy-two days at sea, and a part of the time in great danger from icebergs, we arrived safe in New York, much to the satisfaction of my friends and employer, who all had their fears for our safety. The Sabbath following I was once more favored with an opportunity of meeting my Newark friends, and of making public acknowledgments to Almighty God in his house for his mercies to me while absent. Methinks I experienced peculiar satisfaction in the society of my Christian brethren, with whom of late I had been in habits of so much intimacy, and who seemed to say in their countenances as well as with their lips, Welcome once more in the land of the living.

"Soon after we had delivered the cargo we contemplated another voyage, and as by a late law we were now restricted from going to England, my employers finally concluded to order us for Madeira. Although the difficulties to be expected in our business seemed to be increasing, nevertheless I engaged in this voyage with much less reluctance than was the case the preceding voyage. In general, I trust I can say with sincerity that, notwithstanding the unpleasant sensations at parting with friends, and all the difficulties incident to my situation in life, yet I have found much peace of mind and much of the favor of God; mercies which I desire to feel grateful for, and hope that I may cherish a due sense of my obligations at all times upon my mind.

"Since I have been preparing for this voyage, my thoughts have been much employed on the importance of endeavoring to instruct those who might fall under my care in the great business of religion. I have viewed with concern that this class of men, whose occupation is on the mighty waters, are necessarily excluded from the common opportunities of religious instruction and means of grace with which people on land are favored, and *I could not see how their situation was ever likely to be otherwise, except those who have the command feel it incumbent, and undertake to supply the place of others more capable. And I have often thought our particular situation at sea would greatly assist the feeblest efforts which might be made to lead men to consider their ways.*

"What is better calculated to teach us our dependence on God than to be exposed on the wide ocean, and sometimes in a crazy vessel too, to every gust of wind that blows, and to innumerable dangers which human foresight can not discover, or, if discovered, could not prevent? Is not the mighty power of God remarkably displayed in raising up the stormy wind, which lifteth up the waves thereof, and sometimes threatens destruction to every thing before them? In the 107th Psalm is a grand description of God's power in the deep, and of the situation of those who behold these awful displays. Besides, the sea is particularly favorable to reflection. Called upon for a time to part not only with the most endearing comforts of life, but with those scenes of mirth and folly which drown every serious thought, the sailor, while he stands his watch on deck, is compelled to reflect; and I believe few instances occur where sailors do not feel some secret misgivings for their misspent time while at sea, and resolve to amend their ways.

"And, besides, I have felt accountable to God, in some degree, for the souls of those whom he should put under my care and authority. I did not, indeed, consider myself placed in the situation of a parent, for then, as a professor of religion, I could not have neglected these duties, but rather considered myself as a master and a watchman. I have thought much of the im-port of the words contained in the sixth verse of the thirty-third chapter of Ezekiel. I certainly profess and trust I do see, in some measure, the judgments of God coming upon all finally impenitent sinners; how, then, can I neglect to give them warning, whether they will hear or whether they will forbear, that at least I may deliver my own soul?

"I have also understood the apostle's arguments in the tenth chapter of Romans and fourteenth verse, to be a direction and injunction on all who have the Scriptures in their hands, and hope they understand, in some degree, the will of God as contained therein, to use their influence as they have opportunity, in instructing those who hitherto have remained ignorant or regardless of so important a matter.

"And, if I be not deceived, I see that God is infinitely worthy to be loved by all his intelligent creatures. And do I not believe that *all mankind* are under sin, and have need of a Savior? and shall I be content so long as I secure my own salvation, let what will become of others? Some hints thrown out by the Reverend William Woodbridge, while I was at home, had considerable influence on my mind in determining what ought to be done. But when the various difficulties presented themselves to me—

when I began to count the cost, my resolution began to fail; for I felt wholly insufficient for so great an undertaking, and my own dullness and stupidity rendered me so insensible to the great objects which had now engaged my attention, that I was on the point of giving up the whole as impracticable.

"With all my resolutions and fears before me, I turned my eyes toward the mighty God of Jacob, and resting, I trust, on his promise, that as our day is so shall our strength be, I called the crew together on New-year's day, 1810, and informed them of my intentions, at the same time using arguments to convince them of the necessity and propriety of attending constantly and seriously to the important concerns of religion. They listened to me with apparent readiness to unite in the duties which I had proposed, and accordingly we fixed upon the hour of six o'clock the same evening to meet for these exercises.

"At the time appointed we assembled in the cabin gangway (our cabin being filled with cargo), and spent some time in reading and making some observations on the Scriptures, and concluded with prayer. In the performance of these duties I experienced much less difficulty than I anticipated, and I can say, to the credit of the crew, they all behaved with a very becoming deportment.

"Sabbath, January 7th. Feeling it important that the day set apart for religious worship on shore should be observed in something like such a manner at sea, I made some observations to the crew on the propriety of considering the Sabbath of God's appointment, and as a day set apart for religious worship, and therefore binding on all men and in all places, as circumstances would admit; adding, that it was my desire we should meet at the hour of two o'clock in the afternoon for the purposes before mentioned.

"When the hour arrived we came together, and spent some time in prayer, reading the Scriptures, and something from the works of Mr. Bellamy, &c. While attending to these exercises they all behaved orderly and decent, and, indeed, through the whole day. On the whole, the day has been comfortable to me, far beyond what I have experienced many Sabbaths at sea, and I am not without hopes these feeble attempts to restrain the prevailing vices of those whose business is on the great waters, and to teach the fear of God even in a ship, may not be altogether in vain. Although I dare not say with confidence my motives are pure, and that my actions spring wholly from sincere desires to promote the Redeemer's kingdom, yet sometimes I do hope this is the case.

"Our passage was very comfortable, considering the season of the year, and otherwise much more agreeable than it usually is on board of ships. On the thirty-third day from our leaving New York we were off the town of Funchal (Madeira), and about coming to anchor, but the weather growing squally, we stood to sea again, and the same night came on a heavy gale from the northwest. We returned to the roads again and anchored the eighteenth of January. Found a large number of vessels lying here, a circumstance by no means desirable, it being a wild roadstead at the best. Our cargo being intended for the British market, we were obliged to wait for vessels from England to take it on board. The first fourteen days after our arrival had fine weather, and met with no difficulty; but from this time until we took our departure from the island, we were obliged to put to sea five different times, and on the last of these occasions we were out twenty-three days. Several of our crew got hurt in one way or another, but none proved fatal."

April 7th, having completed discharging the cargo, they sailed for the Cape de Verd Islands for a cargo of salt; but, being disappointed in obtaining it, they proceeded at once in ballast to New York. In reviewing this voyage, he says, "With respect to any effect produced on the crew by attending religious duties, I think I can say with truth, that in general they behaved much less immoral, and for the most part more orderly and decent in their conduct than is usually the case on board of ships, and one of them, a native of Sweden, gave considerable evidence, on his return home, of his having experienced the power of religion on his heart.

"We were not long in port at this time before our employers concluded to send the ship to Liverpool, and, with this view, commenced loading with all possible dispatch. It now appeared advisable for me to acquaint some one of the clergy in the city with my proceedings, and, should they be approved of, to ask further advice and assistance. I saw Dr. Romeyne. He encouraged me to continue the practice, and promised to procure some Bibles from the New York Bible Society, to be disposed of on board as I might deem proper; he also recommended me to get some religious tracts, to be distributed among the crew as occasion might offer. And now the time drew near that I must part with connections and friends, with the society of Christians, and, I may add, almost with the world, to pursue my occupation again on the deep. But this reflection calmed my mind: The Lord is every where—myself and all that is dear to me are in his hands; and with gratitude I can say I don't recollect an instance when I have been so composed on these occasions.

"We were now again a little family of strangers, formed promiscuously of different characters, and about one half of our number were colored people. Sabbath morning, July 8th, being the first opportunity which offered, I called the crew together, and, after entreating them to observe a decency of conduct, to refrain from profane and unbecoming language, and to regard the Sabbath day differently from what is usually the case at sea, I informed them it was my desire we should meet together as often as circumstances would admit to attend upon religious duties after the manner which we had done the voyage before. I also distributed the Bibles among them, as they were destitute, with the religious tracts. I have the pleasure to say, on all occasions when the crew have been called upon to attend on religious exercises, their conduct would have done honor to a better-informed society, and I am not without hopes the Lord will bless these means to the good of some. Wednesday, July 18th, being about the Banks of Newfoundland, we fell in with a large island of ice, appearing to be at least forty feet above the surface of the water. This makes the fourth time I have fallen in with ice in these latitudes; and I can not but remark the interposition of Providence in our escapes from shipwreck, since we have always had thick blowing weather just before we have seen them, after which the weather continued fine until we considered ourselves out of danger.

"My thoughts at this time are dwelling much on the deceitfulness of my own heart. I find that by nature it is desperately wicked; who can know it? And it is astonishing what pleas Satan and corrupt nature will urge that sin may be indulged. But where sin abounded, grace did much more abound. Thanks be to God, the consolations of his word are equal to our wants; herein I found relief to my mind under these fears and doubts from the following passage in the 119th Psalm and 49th verse: 'Remember the word unto thy servant, upon which thou hast caused me to hope.' I find nothing in the Scriptures spoken particularly to me as a foundation to build my hopes upon, but I find there, 'God so loved the world, that he gave his only-begotten Son, that whosoever believeth on him might not perish, but obtain everlasting life;' and, indeed, the whole Bible is calculated to afford consolation and support to the mourner for sin."

On their return from Liverpool, a sudden and awful tempest was experienced, respecting which we find it entered in the Journal: "This I reckoned the third heaviest gale ever witnessed by me. Our ship lay very safe, notwithstanding she would *sometimes roll the fore-yard six feet under water.* As soon as we had secured the sails I called the crew down into the cabin, and sought by prayer and supplication the protection of Him who holdeth the winds in His fists and the waters in the hollow of His hand; and blessed be His name, we were delivered from all evil in this difficult time. Oh that men would praise the Lord for his goodness and for his wonderful works to the children of men."

In another voyage to England, immediately subsequent to this, he took the same course with respect to the Sabbath on the first Lord's day out of port, distributing Bibles and tracts as before, and addressing his crew on the duties of religion; and he remarks, in recording it, "I must now take notice of a circumstance which I can not but deem as providential. Previous to my undertaking to perform religious exercises on board, I had for some considerable time been subject to a great weakness of the lungs, insomuch that I found it difficult to read or speak even for a few minutes; but, from the first attempt until the present time, I have found no difficulty on this account, though I have sometimes been engaged reading and speaking two hours together. On the afternoon of the Sabbath above alluded to, we met and attended to reading the Scriptures, a hymn, something from the confession of faith on prayer, and also Watts's guide to prayer on the same subject, and concluded with prayer.

"Although most part of the crew were strangers to me, and strangers to such proceedings at sea, they conducted with the strictest propriety and good order, and I am now fully convinced *that the notion which many masters and officers of ships entertain, that sailors can not be governed without rough usage and bad language, is altogether void of weight; since I have found, by considerable experience, much less difficulty in the matter than when, as formerly (with shame I confess it), I have myself used these practices.* And it is also a mistake that sailors will mock at every thing like religion on board. It is true that some appear to be very little affected with its weighty concerns, and is it not true, also, that many discover the same indifference on land?"

On their return from Bristol they took on board a number of passengers both in the cabin and steerage; and with the Christian fidelity and carefulness for souls which had now become a part of Captain Congar's character, he took occasion, as soon as they were over their sea-sickness, to express his wish that they should attend to religious duties on Sabbath days, and on the evening of every day. This, he says, they all readily assented to, and some of them even seemed desirous of it.

"One of the passengers in the steerage, being a professor of religion, used to assist on these occasions, and this practice we continued all the passage, and it was not only comfortable to myself, but I hope in some measure profitable to all. The latter part of the passage we had more favorable winds, and arrived in New York July 13th, being forty-four days, all in good health; for which mercies I desire to be thankful, but especially for the consolations of the Spirit afforded me at different times while at sea, so that I trust I could say His favor is life, and his loving-kindness is better than life."

This habit he continued in successive voyages to and from England until the interruption of commerce with Great Britain by the war of 1812. The inconvenience of being put out of business thereby, he gratefully takes notice, was made up to him by the satisfaction found in the society of friends and Christian ordinances. At the Lord's Supper he had humbling views of his own unworthiness, and reviving views of Christ, that made him exclaim,

> Why was I made to hear thy voice,
> And enter while there's room,
> While thousands make a wretched choice,
> And rather starve than come.

"Having, therefore, professedly set to my seal that God is true, oh that I might be enabled to dedicate myself to His service. Surely his service is an easy service. It is perfect freedom. His yoke is easy and his burden is light. Have I not found by experience that the service of God is easier than the service of sin and Satan, without regard to consequences? Awake, then, my sluggish soul, trim up thy lamp, and be like them that wait for their Lord, when he shall return from the wedding.

"It would surpass my powers to mention

the tender mercies of God toward me since I have been at home with my friends. Much I have enjoyed in their society and that of my Christian brethren.

"It now became my duty to resume my profession. The state of war in which our nation was unhappily engaged with Great Britain, together with the difficulty which we were liable to on the ocean from the armed vessels of other nations, particularly the Algerines, who had lately declared hostilities against the United States, rendered this business extremely hazardous. But, believing that my duty lay in that line, and endeavoring to commit my way unto the Lord, who is always ready to relieve the wants of his dependent creatures, I went to New York for the purpose of seeking employ. I had been in the city but a few days before I met with Mr. N., my late employer, who gave me to understand he was about preparing the ship Susannah for a voyage to Lisbon, and intimated a wish I should take charge of her. This I readily agreed to, and on the 18th of October commenced my new engagements on board the above ship.

"Without interruption from the cruisers of any nation, we passed the Azores in twenty days, on the 11th of December made the Rock of Lisbon, and at 3 P.M. of the next day came to anchor in the Tagus, all well. While lying here, a heavy blow from the westward did great damage to the shipping. Several were obliged to slip or cut their cables and run on shore, in order to avoid greater damage; and two drifted down with the ebb tide, and, for want of cables and anchors, were totally lost. Providentially," says Captain Congar, "we escaped with trifling injury. From the commencement of the voyage we have been accustomed to the practice of attending religious duties as often as possible, and I am happy to say on these occasions the crew have generally behaved with great decorum and regularity. But, alas! what stupidity and coldness is but too manifest among us. For my own part, I am constrained to acknowledge that, after all my professions and attainments, all my resolutions and hopes, if the spirit of grace should withdraw from me, I am undone; and I feel convinced that heaven can never be attained by my own strength or wisdom. Oh Lord! preserve me from that lukewarmness, and its dreadful consequences, with which the Church of the Laodiceans are charged, and for which they are threatened; and warm my heart with the Savior's love, that I may not merely possess the form of godliness while destitute of the power thereof. Oh for the constant witness of the Spirit that I am born of God! Let my hope of heaven be steady and bright, then will I hold on in the way of obedience, and wax stronger and stronger."

THROUGH night, and clouds, and gloomy fears,
  Though dragons often roar,
Yet in the great Redeemer's strength
  I'll press to Canaan's shore.
Methinks I now begin to see
  The borders of that land;
The trees of grace with heavenly fruit
  In beauteous order stand:
The wint'ry time will soon be gone,
  The summer soon appear;
The glorious day is rolling on,
  The great Sabbatic year.
Oh! what a glorious sight appears
  To my believing eyes;
Methinks I see Jerusalem,
  A city in the skies.
Oh! that my faith were strong to rise,
  And bear my soul away,
I'd give all glory to the Lamb,
  Through everlasting day.

Chapter VII.

CHRISTIAN LIFE AND DUTIES AT SEA CONTINUED.

Bought by Christ's blood, and to the purchase true,
The Christian runs with cheerfulness the race
Which God in wisdom hath seen fit to trace,
Nor turns, some other object to pursue;
Nor slacks his steadfast course; sometimes he sees
Fires in his path, or hears the serpent's breath,
Or raging men with implements of death,
But still goes on, nor like the coward flees.
The road is strait and narrow; if he turns,
Ruin awaits him; if he onward goes,
With face erect and heart with love that burns,
However great the obstacles, he knows
That God, who hath all power, all things can do,
Will guard him in his straits, and bear him glorious through.

Scripture Sonnets.

Early in the year 1813 we find Captain Congar again in command on the deep, keeping the Sabbath day holy before his crew, and so acting as their minister and friend as to secure their good-will and hearty concurrence in his measures for sanctifying the Lord's day. His voyages were in a high degree successful, escaping both the ordinary dangers of the sea and those from hostile privateers and cruisers. He returned to share in the remarkable work of grace which was then in progress through New Jersey and other parts of the Middle States. He entered into it with great delight, and a manifest refreshing to his own soul, remarking respecting it, "Thus are the walls of the spiritual Jerusalem building up even in troublesome times."

But he was not now to enjoy it long, for his employer soon informed him of his intention to dispatch the ship again to Lisbon. "I could have wished," he says, "to have stayed a little longer with my family and friends, and the people of God, but I endeavored to submit to the will of Providence, trusting that all things were ordered in wisdom and in mercy.

"Friday, April 9th, our ship being loaded, and seeing but little prospect of getting out to sea before the Sabbath, my mind became concerned to know how far it would be consistent with the command to remember the Sabbath day to keep it holy, to proceed on the voyage should a favorable wind offer on the Sabbath. My mind had been more or less exercised on this subject for a long time past, and I had come to this conclusion, that when no unavoidable occurrence made it necessary, we ought by all means to refuse commencing the voyage on that day, which was not only set apart as a day of worship, but as a day of rest from worldly concerns, *that thy man-servant and thy maid-servant may rest as well as thou.*

"Sabbath morning arrived, the wind was favorable, and my employer anxious, fearing a blockade from the British, we proceeded. But, as though the Lord intended to show us that our exertions and anxieties were fruitless, when we reached Sandy Hook the wind became unfavorable, and continued so three days. I now had time to reflect upon what we had done, and from the reasons enjoined in the Scriptures, my own feelings on the subject, and the remonstrances of conscience, I formed this resolve, *that, through the assistance of divine grace, should I ever have the command of a ship offered me again, I would, at the same time, give my employer to understand my determination not to commence the voyage on a day clearly instituted by divine wisdom for the most exalted employment of which man is capable.*

"The same evening we left the city, we commenced attending religious duties as on other voyages; and although on each voyage some part of the crew were strangers to me and strangers to such a practice, yet they manifested a readiness to unite in these duties, which could scarcely have been expected." This was a speedy and successful voyage, and they sailed again from the Tagus, homeward bound, June 4th. "We had all been very healthy while in port, but, shortly after sailing, almost every one of the crew complained of bad colds, attended with soreness of the throat and pains in the bones; and, among the rest, I had an attack of the same, the nature of which assumed the character of the influenza as nearly as any other complaint. Oh, may these light afflictions, which are but for a moment, work for us a far more exceeding and eternal weight of glory. How very just are the remarks of an ancient poet on the good of evils:

> One week's extremity may teach us more
> Than long prosperity had done before;
> Death is forgotten in our easy state,
> But troubles mind us of our final fate;
> The doing ill affects us not with fears,
> But suffering ill brings sorrow, woe, and tears.

"It is not easy to reflect that we are mortal, dying creatures; that we are liable every moment to be crushed before the moth when prosperity, health, and ease attend us constantly. How salutary, then, are afflictions. Herein we learn our absolute and entire dependence on God for all things, even those mercies which by reason of their commonness we too often overlook. Herein do we realize the vanity of sublunary enjoyments, and how little comfort they can administer in a time of trouble, and thus, through divine grace, are we enabled to seek a portion in a better world. Nothing so effectually writes vanity on all things beneath the sun as afflictions. Yet there is a real good in possessing health, wealth, and the varied and multiplied comforts of a kind Providence. The great evil arises from our abuse of, or an inordinate attachment to these gifts, which were not designed as the best portion Infinite Love had to give; and it would be as inconsistent for us to consider temporary enjoyments any thing more than transient comforts afforded us while passing through the journey of life to the haven of rest, as it would be for the traveler to sit down contented with the first commodious inn he might stop at, and say I am fully satisfied with what I find here, and so make no further attempts to prosecute his way, though immense wealth was ready for him at his journey's end.

"Methinks I can now join the Psalmist and say, 'It was good for me that I was afflicted.' One great mercy it would be the highest ingratitude in me not to remember and acknowledge. The Lord has graciously been pleased to afford me pretty generally, during my present trouble, a comfortable sense of his Divine favor. I have not felt over-anxious about the issue of this disease: I trust I feel in good measure willing the Lord should do with me as seemeth good in his sight. I am entirely in his hands, and I have no claim on goodness or mercy. Every comfort I receive, and every hope afforded me, I consider gratuitously free and undeserved. But alas! how many errors and imperfections do I discover in my heart and life. Affliction brings about, as it were, a sort of court of inquiry into all our actions. This we approve, and that we condemn, and we discover many failings which otherwise would never have been detected.

"Thursday, June 17th. Through the infinite kindness of Him who restores the sick and preserves the health of his dependent creatures, we are all again comfortable, and favored with winds and pleasant weather, each one hoping soon to meet his friends on the shores of Columbia. May it be the sincere and unreserved language of every heart on board, 'What shall I render to the Lord for all his benefits?' June 27th. This day I have entered upon the forty-sixth year of my life. Not to examine what I have been doing the whole period of my existence, let me glance over my temper and conduct the years just past, if by these means I may discover whether I have gone forward in the divine life, or whether I must be constrained to draw the unfavorable conclusion of the reverse. And here I not only have to lament my dullness, and shortcomings, and unprofitableness in the things of religion, but, in too many instances, by my temper and behavior, I fear that I have given occasion for the enemies of religion to speak reproachfully. But the Lord's mercies exceed our faults. With gratitude I desire to acknowledge the kindness and patience of God toward me in bearing with my infirmities, and affording me so many instances of his fatherly care, in watching over my life and health, and bringing me to the commencement of a new era of my existence in circumstances of comfort beyond my deserts, and so far beyond what so many of my fellow-creatures enjoy: 'Bless the Lord, O my soul! and forget not all his benefits.'

"And now, since through that same mercy and goodness which I have been the subject of from the day of my birth am I again entered upon a new period of my mortal life, what engagements does it behoove me to make; what resolutions to form? Surely I ought to love the Lord with all my might and strength. Every faculty should be swift to do his will. May I then go on, in the strength of my Redeemer, to every work allotted me, taking up my cross daily. Oh that I might learn habitually to deny myself, to subdue every corrupt passion, and thus be preparing for the society of those blessed spirits who, with one heart and voice, cease not to cry, 'Holy, holy is the Lord of hosts; the whole earth is full of thy glory.' Oh, when shall I be there with them!"

By faith I see the land,
The port of endless rest:
My soul, thy sails expand,
And fly to Jesus's breast!
Oh, may I reach the heavenly shore,
Where winds and waves distress no more!

On their return from Lisbon, being warned by a frigate and privateer, fallen in with east of Halifax, not to attempt New York or the Sound, they put in to Newport. In the small town of Somerset, not far from there, the ship was laid up and crew discharged, the prosecution of the war forbidding any farther commerce. For eighteen months Captain Congar was now at home, enjoying highly the religious privileges with which he was favored, and finding them eminently conducive to his edification. In order that he might be useful at the same time, he opened a school at his own house, which he continued teaching until the middle of February, 1815, when we find it thus entered in the journal: "A messenger arrived from England with a treaty of peace between Great Britain and the United States, concluded at Ghent, and ratified by the British government. This gratifying news was received throughout the United States with the most lively sensibility, and by many with devout thankfulness.

"I now began to turn my thoughts once more toward the sea, and in a few days received a letter from my late employers giving me to understand they had a ship, the command of which I might have as soon as the ice should dissolve so that she could be brought down the river (being then at Poughkeepsie, about eighty miles above New York). Having dismissed my school, I proceeded on my way, the eighteenth of March, to take charge of the ship Niagara, the ice in the river being principally broken up. In about a week we returned to New York with the ship, and almost immediately began preparing to sail for New Orleans. As I had done before, so soon as circumstances opened a way, I introduced the practice of attending religious worship on the Sabbath, having a number of passengers, and also distributed some Bibles among the crew, supplied me by the Auxiliary Bible Society of New York, and several religious tracts."

They reached New Orleans safely on the eleventh of June, and left again for Liverpool on the twenty-eighth, "happy in the prospect of being not only relieved from the oppression of the heat, but from being annoyed by the musketoes, which, for the time we were coming down the river, seemed almost insupportable.

"Soon after being at sea, I informed the crew it was *my intention to attend religious worship morning and evening of every day when the weather and other circumstances would permit*, giving them to understand, at the same time, that I wished them to feel perfectly at liberty to attend on these occasions, or to omit if they thought proper, recommending to them, however, the diligent use of the means of grace as the most likely way to obtain the pardon of sin, and insure the Divine blessing on the work of our hands.

"Sometimes I would take opportunity to exhort them to repentance and to forsake their sins, endeavoring to show them, in my feeble manner, the dreadfulness of lying under the curse of God, and recommending religion as the only thing to prepare us to live or die, setting forth the reasonableness of the Divine commands, and the wickedness and folly of rebelling against the God of heaven and earth. The Lord is a sovereign; with him I desire to leave my endeavors to promote religion among my fellow-seamen. If he should see fit to make me an instrument of good to any who sail with me, to his name be all the glory.

"Friday, July 28th. This birth-day my soul is bowed down under a sense of my sin, and I go mourning all the day. Alas! for my follies the past year. But oh! the mercies bestowed by a covenant God. How many of my countrymen have fallen in battle; how many families have been driven from their homes; how many suffered to run into evils and temptations, while I have been preserved and delivered from the snare of the fowler. Divine Savior, keep me still by thy power, through faith unto salvation. But oh! my inconstant heart! What abundant reason have I to distrust it? Surely it is deceitful above all things, and desperately wicked; who can know it? What a wonder of grace that I am spared. Oh Lord, give me not only repentance for all my sins, but give me faith in thy blood, that I may always apply to that all-sufficient fountain, wash, and be clean."

They reached Liverpool safely, but soon after leaving for New York a heavy gale overtook them, during which they found it difficult to keep off the land. "In this perilous time," says Captain Congar, "I called the crew together, expressed to them my fears for our safety, and besought them to join me in imploring mercy and Divine protection from shipwreck; and, blessed be that God whose ears are always open to the cries of the needy who put their trust in him, we were saved from all our fears. The winds moderated and became more favorable, and we proceeded on our way."

The ensuing winter of 1815–16 was spent at home; but in June Captain Congar is put in charge of the ship Phocion by his old employers, and dispatched to Lisbon and St. Ubes, whither he takes his wife with him, and arrives back from a successful voyage on the twenty-sixth of September, 1816. At its close he says, "According to our usual practice, we attended our religious duties on board, and I hope not without some good effect. The crew, when paid off, very liberally put into my hands thirteen dollars for the New York Bible Society."

Immediately after discharging cargo, the Phocion was ordered again to Wilmington, North Carolina, and thence to Hull, England. On the passage we find this entry: "Sabbath,

April 13th, 1817. This day, the weather being fine, we had a more favorable opportunity to attend religious duties than usual. According to my imperfect manner, I read the Scriptures, exhorted, admonished, and prayed with my crew. They attended with decency of conduct; and I still hope, through the Divine mercy, that my feeble efforts to be some way useful to my fellow-seamen will not be altogether in vain. But oh, my soul, what art thou doing? Thou teachest others; teachest thou not thyself? I am indeed in heaviness through manifold temptations. 'Oh Lord, undertake for me, and deliver me; so shall I praise thy name.'

"Friday, 18th. Oh! how shall sinners stand at the bar of God to answer for the deeds done in the body? 'If my heart condemn me, God is greater than my heart, and knoweth all things.' How little do we know of ourselves, except the Spirit of truth open our eyes to see the extent of the Divine commands, and to see what a holy Being we have to do with. If I were called to an account for my neglects of duty to my fellow-creatures, what could I answer? Alas! how numberless have been my failures. How unfaithful to my wife, in not admonishing with meekness, how little concerned for her everlasting welfare. I am distressed lest she should perish through my criminal indifference for her soul's salvation. Oh, how little charity, how little true benevolence for men! How faint my zeal for the Redeemer's kingdom, except the Divine life be maintained in the soul. 'Woe to them that are at ease in Zion, that trust in the mountain of Samaria.' Too long have I been at ease, and trusted in my own righteousness.

"How dangerous is prosperity, either in temporal or spiritual things. 'Surely I am more brutish than any man, and have not the understanding of a man.' O Lord, if prosperity cause me to wander from thee, let me never have prosperity while I live. Keep me by thy grace in the valley of humiliation. Deep humility best becomes so great a sinner. Oh, rather let me go softly all my years, in the bitterness of my soul, than that I should be lifted up with spiritual pride, and forget God. April 24th. I am made to feel that sin is a great evil, and to realize that the Lord is a God of knowledge, and by him actions are weighed. How desirable is it to have a comfortable sense that our sins are forgiven; but, alas for me! what right have I to look for comfort? My backslidings reprove me, and I am made to possess the iniquities of my youth. The precious volume of inspiration is, indeed, full of condescending and gracious invitations to sinners to return to their offended Sovereign. I would endeavor, through Divine assistance, still to hope in the mercy of God through Jesus Christ. Blessed be his name that we read that he came to save them who, through fear of death, were all their lifetime subject to bondage, and that he suffered, being tempted, that he might succor them that are tempted."

"CLEANSE me, O Lord, and cheer my soul
With thy forgiving love;
O make my broken spirit whole,
And bid my pains remove.
Let not thy Spirit quite depart,
Nor drive me from thy face;
Create anew my vicious heart,
And fill it with thy grace.
Then will I make thy mercy known
Before the sons of men;
Backsliders shall address thy throne,
And turn to God again."

CHAPTER VIII.

PECULIAR RELIGIOUS EXERCISES AND ORIGINAL CORRESPONDENCE WITH REV. THOMAS SCOTT.

THUS from the Elect, regenerate through faith,
Pass the dark passions, and what thirsty cares
Drink up the spirit. Lo! they vanish, or acquire
New names, new features—by supernal grace
Enrobed with light, and naturalized in heaven.
  Who feeds and saturates his soul with love,
  He from his small particular orbit flies
  With bless'd outstarting! From himself he flies,
  Stands in the sun, and with no partial gaze
  Views all creation: and he loves it all,
  And blesses it, and calls it very good!

COLERIDGE.

THE year 1817, while it was distinguished in the religious annals of America for the extraordinary working of the Holy Spirit throughout the churches, was a year of great heart-searching and anxiety for souls on the part of Captain Congar. He seems to have been exercised with very affecting views of the sinfulness of sin, and the holiness of God, and the fearful liability of the soul in a state of condemnation. The burden of souls often lay like a mountain of iron upon his own breast. His anxiety for the salvation of his wife, who was not one with him in the hopes, and joys, and desires of the Christian, was, as it will appear in this chapter, deep and absorbing, while it was altogether sober and rational, and set him upon the use of proper means of grace and awakening.

On the twenty-fifth of April we find the following entry in his journal, being at sea: "This day my soul is full of heaviness, my heart within me is desolate. If this be the fruit of sin in this life, oh how dreadful to lay under the weight of God's wrath through an endless eternity! and yet it would be just for me to be dealt with in this awful manner. If I be saved, what a monument of mercy! what a miracle of grace! How often has the language of my heart been, in its pride, such as this, 'That I am rich, and increased in goods, and have need of nothing; and knew not that I was wretched, and miserable, and poor, and blind, and naked.' But the glorious Redeemer," says he, "'stands at the door and knocks; and if any man hear his voice and open the door, he will come in to him, and sup with him, and he shall sup with me.' Oh! may my heart be opened to receive the heavenly guest, and may he abide with me, and may I abide in him. But ah! the deceitfulness of the human heart; I only know that I am anxiously seeking to be delivered from the burden of sin. But here again I am encouraged; the blessed Savior says, 'The whole need not a physician, but they that are sick. I came not to call the righteous, but sinners to repentance.'"

Here follow a course of letters to Mrs. Congar, written on ship-board, when travailing with desire for her soul.

"At sea, March 25th, 1817.

"My dear Wife,—The emotions of my heart, excited by our late parting, under circumstances somewhat afflicting, have caused deep anxiety in my soul for your present and future welfare. Were I to strive, I could not erase from my mind those solemn scenes which I have witnessed within a few months past. You have indeed been an afflicted woman for a course of years, but, in some instances of late, your distress appeared next to insupportable. You seemed like one in a perfect agony; your expressions of horror, your cries for mercy, the convulsions of your body, rent my very soul, while I endeavored to supplicate the throne of grace in your behalf.

"And now, O my dear wife, how can I prove a sincere regard for your good better than by entreating you earnestly to consider what you should do? You have seen how easy it would be for the Lord to cut you off. You have had numberless instances of frailty, and must we not allow that sin is the procuring cause of all our sufferings? You may, indeed, live many years, but it can not be looked for according to the course of things. Your constitution and health are so far impaired, and you are subject to such violent and complicated disorders, that it often appears to me like a miracle that you have survived such dreadful shocks, and yet live. I beseech you, therefore, no longer delay the great concerns of your immortal soul.

"You have been deeply afflicted about your situation in the time of your distress. Your language was such as the following: 'If I was prepared to die, I should not wish to live one moment; but oh! I am not prepared to die. Father of mercies, Father of mercies, spare me; have mercy on me! O that I was prepared to die. (Addressing yourself to me), Can you do nothing for me? I must die;' and such like.

"You know that something is necessary to be done to fit you to die; but you do not know how long space of repentance will be granted. The Lord Jesus is willing and able to save any sinner who will come to him with a broken heart. If you find your heart is hard and unhumbled, beg of him to give you a new heart, and to not leave you to yourself and the temptations of Satan. We do need his blood to cleanse us from all our sins. If you die in your sins, where he is you can not come. And oh! what mortal on this side eternity can conceive how dreadful it will be to possess a heart at enmity with God and all holy beings forever, and to be a companion of devils and wicked spirits. If we could not endure the society of some disagreeable character a day or an hour, how could we endure to be shut up to all eternity with those we hate, and where there is nothing but weeping, and wailing, and gnashing of teeth?

"But I forbear. You are highly favored with the means of grace, and you have many pious friends with whom you may converse. Although I have been sadly negligent in the things of religion, yet I firmly believe nothing else can afford true happiness here, or secure our peace with God beyond the grave. I am now going three thousand miles from you. We can not fathom the dispensations of Providence. Whether we shall be permitted to see each other's face in the land of the living is to us unknown. I beg you, then, not to take offense at what I have hinted, but accept it as a token of my affectionate regard for your peace and happiness. I feel much for you. I endeavor to pray for you. May the Lord grant you mercy, for his name's sake."

"Thursday, March 27th.

"MY DEAR WIFE,—What can I do better than write you, who, though absent in body, yet are present in mind? I am sensible of your case. It calls for compassion. You have read the lives of martyrs. You see how triumphantly they left this vain world. The sting of death was taken away. They had no fears beyond the grave. They even longed to depart when they knew that they were to be thrown to the wild beasts. The grace of the Lord Jesus made them what they were; and he is as ready now to give his grace to any who will seek it with humility, as in those days of martyrdom.

"We need this divine principle. The whole soul must be renovated. The heart must be purified by faith. We must have a relish for heavenly things. And we need not, like Dives, desire that one might be sent from the dead to show to us the realities of the invisible world. We have better testimony in the Bible than any mere man could give. In that precious volume, while sinners are warned against the danger of perishing through obstinate unbelief, they are encouraged to apply for mercy through the great Redeemer's blood.

"Oh! let not Satan tempt you to despondency. It is one of his devices to ruin souls. Desponding melanoholy will never save us, though we should indulge it to all eternity. We want no other evidence than the Bible affords that the Lord is gracious, willing, and able to save, even those who have sinned against him until the eleventh hour. Such is the grace of the Gospel that none need despair. The blessed Savior has a compassionate heart. It was this that moved him to die for sinners, and he has not promised more than he will perform. He says, 'Come unto me, all ye that are weary and heavy laden, and I will give you rest.'

"But oh! how hard is it to humble ourselves before God. How long will the rebellious temper of fallen man refuse to submit? May we remember that we can not contend against an Almighty arm and prosper. We shall be constrained to submit willingly, and be happy, or unwillingly, and be miserable.

"Now is the time he bends his ear,
And waits for your request;
Come, lest he rouse his wrath, and swear
You shall not see my rest.

"Thursday, April 3d.

"MY DEAR WIFE,—From the fullness of my heart I write. I tremble to think of the solemn circumstances in which we are. I beseech you, let not the long-suffering and patience of God induce you to put far off eternal things. You know that for several years I have been a professor of religion. You have seen me in great distress of mind, and, again, you have witnessed my joy, as I then trusted in God my Savior. But oh! my sins have separated between God and my soul, and I often fear I have been deceiving myself. We have now lived in the marriage relation more than twenty years. Alas! how little have we done for each other's everlasting welfare. As we are united in the bonds of matrimony, we ought to have been united in serving God. We are in a world of sin and temptation. We need each other's counsel, we need each other's prayers.

"I hope and pray these lines may find you in health. If so, be not flattered thereby. Health is precarious. Improve it to prepare for a time of affliction, and to prepare for death. We can not live without the favor of God. We can only look for this by deep and humble repentance for all our sins, and an unfeigned faith in the blessed Redeemer. It is matter of everlasting praise that the great Jehovah should condescend to invite such rebellious creatures to return to him. Rather might he not justly have left us to perish without hope? Why, then, should we slight such love and grace?

"Every thing has been done that was necessary to open a way for God to be propitious to our fallen race. What can we promise ourselves from sin or the world? Have we not seen enough to satisfy us that we must not look here for true enjoyment? Were our hearts right with God, we should take a sacred pleasure in contemplating his divine glories and perfections. His commandments would not be burdensome and grievous. The angels in heaven take a sacred pleasure in serving their Creator, and ought not we of the footstool to esteem it our highest privilege to be thus employed?

"But ah! we have a body of sin and death. This must be mortified; our corrupt passions be regulated, our wills subdued, and our whole souls transformed into the image of God. We must be born again.

"Oh! then, let us give ourselves no rest or peace until we can entertain some rational hope that our sins are pardoned, and our names written in the Lamb's book of life.

"Sunday, April 13th.

"My dear Wife,—Though ignorant of what has befallen you since we parted, I still hope, by this time, you are returned safe to the bosom of your connections and friends. If so, reflect on the goodness and mercy of God in sparing your life, preserving you from the perils of the deep, succoring you under your sore afflictions, and restoring you to the society of your dear friends once more. And while your soul is filled with gratitude for these temporal mercies, oh! ponder with humble admiration on the greatness of that grace which moved the counsels of eternal wisdom to provide a ransom for sinners.

"You are in a place highly favored with the blessings of the Gospel, and this is a day of the Lord's merciful visitation. He is, no doubt, calling many who have long been the subjects of Satan into his kingdom! Oh! let us fear, lest a promise being left us of entering into his rest, we should come short of it. Consider that by nature we have evil hearts of unbelief, prone to depart from the living God, and that we can not return to him by our own strength.

"Time is precious, and our souls are of infinite value. What if our whole lives had been spent in the service of our Maker, we should have done but our duty, and we should have suffered no loss, for wisdom's ways are ways of pleasantness. The yoke of Christ is easier to bear than the yoke of Satan. Satan is a hard master. He oppresses and destroys his subjects; but Christ protects, supports, and comforts them which belong to his kingdom, and will finally conduct them to never-ending felicity.

"But, alas for me! how often have I willingly subjected myself to the service of Satan. Why was I seduced by the great deceiver? I lament my follies past, and I would mourn over them; but I must remember that my repentance can not make amends. I never can pay the debt which I have contracted. If Christ be my surety and pay the debt, I shall have a discharge; my sins and iniquities will be remembered no more against me; if otherwise, I must pay the debt by everlasting torments. May the mercy of God be extended, that I may not come into this condemnation!

"My dear Mary,—I often feel deeply distressed in my mind lest I should never be permitted to see your face again in the land of the living. I have been so unfaithful, have done so little for your everlasting interest, and in many instances, I fear, have done much to prejudice your mind against religion. Have I lived only to harden you in sin? We have traveled together many leagues over the boundless ocean, and have seen much of the wonders of God in the deep. Why have we not been excited thereby to strive more to serve God and seek each other's happiness? In the light of eternity we shall discover things very different from what we now do. Oh, I beseech you, recollect the scenes we have passed through, reflect upon the goodness of God, and seek first of all his kingdom and righteousness, and all other things shall be added unto you.

"Friday, April 18th.

"MY DEAR WIFE,—Oh, how shall sinners stand at the bar of God to answer for the deeds done in the body? 'If our hearts condemn us, God is greater than our hearts, and knoweth all things.' How little do we know of ourselves, except the Spirit of truth open our eyes to see the extent of the Divine command, and to see what a holy Being we have to do with. If we were called to an account for our neglects of duty to each other and to our fellow-creatures, what could we answer? Alas! how numberless have been our failures; how little true benevolence to man; how infinite our shortcomings to God.

"I deeply bewail my want of charity to you,

and the many instances of my conduct which, I fear, have been a stumbling-block to you and others. But let us leave the things that are behind, and press toward the mark for the prize of the high calling of God in Christ Jesus. I have written to you briefly and but in part of my thoughts concerning you. Your sore afflictions have excited my tenderest sympathy. Could I now be certain you are once more returned to the bosom of your friends, perhaps my anxieties would in some degree abate; but still you would be in the hands of a just God, who marks all our ways, and whose long-suffering will not always bear with our sins. Oh, then, return to him and make your peace, and thereby good shall come unto thee.

"What an invaluable treasure is the volume of inspiration. The whole tenor of its language is, 'Let the wicked forsake his way, and the unrighteous man his thoughts; and let him return unto the Lord, and he will have mercy upon him, and to our God, for he will abundantly pardon.' I was particularly struck with the condescending and gracious manner in which sinners are invited to return to their offended Sovereign by the Prophet Jeremiah, in the third chapter and first verse: 'They say if a man put away his wife, and she go from him and become another man's, shall he return unto her again? Shall not that land be greatly polluted? But thou hast played the harlot with many lovers; yet return again to me, saith the Lord.'

"And, moreover, he expostulates with us in the most kind and endearing language: 'Oh, my people, what have I done unto thee? and wherein have I wearied thee? Testify against me.'

"Why are such methods used to bring rebellious sinners back to God? Why should we be treated thus? We can only say because the Lord's ways are higher than our ways, as the heavens are above the earth. Methinks I never before had such solemn reflections on the importance of the marriage relation with reference to eternity as I now have. How seldom do we consider that our conduct toward each other will be the means of promoting our everlasting felicity or enhancing our never-ending woe. We too often live as though we were to have no existence beyond the grave. Is it not to be feared that many a day has passed since our connection without ever once entertaining a single thought about each other's salvation? How seldom do we consider the importance of example. Alas! how much idle conversation. May the Lord forgive, and, if we be spared to meet again, enable us to act more consistently with our mutual engagements, and with the duties which we owe to our great Creator.

"How different has been our conduct to each other from what is enjoined by the apostle to the Ephesians, 5th chapter, from the 21st verse to the end, and in the 3d chapter, first epistle of Peter, from the beginning to the 9th verse. Have we not too much reason to lament deeply our want of meekness, and kindness, and long-suffering, and charity? But oh, where will the catalogue of failures in duty end? We must look to Sovereign grace to pardon and wash away all our faults in the atoning blood of the great Redeemer."

His benevolent care for and sympathy with his passengers appear frequently on his return voyage from Hull with a complement of fifty; and they place the prudent and religious ship-master in an attractive light, and worthy of imitation. Near the close of the passage there is an entry to this effect: "Getting near the land, as we supposed, one of the passengers, a lad named Thomas Jackson, thirteen years of age, went up into the main-top, with a view to look for land, and shortly after fell from thence on deck, and instantly expired. This was an affecting stroke to his aged parents, as he was the only child they had with them, and on whose account principally they had left their native land. It pierced my own heart, and I deeply mourned for them. But God only could bind up the broken heart."

Arrived safely in port, and returning to Newark, he had the pleasure to hear that a very extensive revival of religion had taken place during his absence, so that upward of two hundred and fifty had been added to the different churches in that place; and there were still new cases of awakenings. He prayed with fervor, "May this glorious work continue and spread until the kingdoms and nations of this world shall become the kingdoms and nations of our Lord and of his Christ."

We now turn a leaf in Captain Congar's history that will be perused with no ordinary interest and profit by all conscientious Sabbath-keeping mariners. It opens thus on a voyage to Liverpool, undertaken immediately after his last arrival from Hull:

"Sabbath day, the 7th of September. Last evening the weather had been blowing hard, which obliged us to shorten sail; and as I felt conscientious about making all the sail we could on the Lord's day, the passengers were not a little dissatisfied, which they expressed to me.

I stated to them my reasons for not making the same exertions on the Sabbath days as at other times, but they were no better reconciled.

"Feeling myself at a loss how to act, I endeavored to make my case the subject of prayer; but, not seeing my way entirely clear, I wrote the following letter to an eminent divine in England, intending to forward it on our arrival at Liverpool, being desirous to have the sentiments of one on the subject whom I considered very correct in his expositions of the Scriptures.

"Reverend and dear Sir,—Although I have not the pleasure of being personally acquainted with you, yet, from the high character you sustain in America as an expositor of the sacred Scriptures, and particularly with myself, I have taken the liberty to write you, requesting your opinion on a subject which has long occupied my mind, and which has more than once involved me in some difficulty with my fellow-creatures. I beg leave to inform you, sir, that I am master of an American vessel; that I have been a professor of religion a number of years; and that, since I was first brought to see, in a measure, the extent of the Divine requirements as contained in the ten commandments, I have had many scruples as to the consistency of either engaging myself, or of employing those under my care, in the common transactions of sailing a ship on the Sabbath day.

"I will endeavor to explain my views. I consider the command to keep the Sabbath day holy binding on all men, as well at sea as on land; that it is as necessary one day in seven should be distinguished as a day of religious worship on the deep as on shore, and that this ought always be attended to whenever the weather and other circumstances will permit. I suppose it right to employ our hands in whatever is necessary for the safety of the ship; and, further, that we may so trim our sails, when a change of wind takes place, as to keep the ship as near her destined course as possible. But I do not consider it proper to make the same exertions, by spreading all the canvas possible, to get the ship on her way, which would not only be proper on other days, but absolutely a duty. Some are of opinion that it is right to make the best of a favorable wind when it comes, as well on the Sabbath as on any other day. I can not acknowledge the justness of this principle. I consider, also, the practice of going to sea on the Sabbath a breach of the Divine command, and I have had some disputes with my employer on the subject.

"For several years past I have been in the habit of calling my crew together on the Lord's day to attend religious duties, which I esteem a great privilege. Every kind of unnecessary work, therefore, must break in upon a regular attendance on those duties, and so far do away any impressions which might be excited by attending to the things of religion. I feel deeply sensible I ought to possess a clear judgment of what is duty and what is not, in order that I may not, through conformity to the world or ignorance of the commands of God, habitually and knowingly transgress; or lest I should be more rigid in this respect than the Scriptures enjoin, and thereby become chargeable with being righteous over much, and instead of recommending the religion of the Bible to others, should be the means of prejudicing their minds against it.

"The particular circumstances which gave rise to this letter were the following: On our late passage from New York to this port, it so fell out that we had blowing weather three successive Saturdays, which obliged us to shorten sail; and, as I before observed, I felt conscientious in not ordering more sail to be set on Sabbath morning, which might have been done, and which we should have done on any other day of the week. We had on board three gentlemen passengers, who had noticed that we did not use the same efforts to get along on our way Sabbath days as at other times, and wished to know what I meant; remarking that they were anxious to get to our destined port, and would not submit to such treatment.

"I explained to them my views in the best manner I was capable, but they were no better satisfied; observing that, whatever religious customs I might see fit to introduce in the ship, I ought not to let these things interfere with any exertions to make the best of our way; that it was altogether an uncommon circumstance; and that, had they been acquainted beforehand with my practice in this respect, they would not have taken passage with us.

"I did not immediately comply with their wishes; but, about noon, the wind was favorable, and fine weather, and discovering one of the passengers in a great passion, I thought it best to order more sail to be set. We did not, indeed, set all sail possible; but my heart smote me, and my conscience is hurt. I have offended them, and, I have reason to fear, offended my Almighty judge. One of the gentlemen observed to me that, if I considered work done on board the ship as a breach of the Sabbath, to be consistent, I ought to have all the sails furled on Saturday, and lay by until Monday morning; and, indeed, that if I would keep it strictly, I must not follow the water business at all.

"You will perceive, sir, how difficult I must find it to preserve good order in the ship, as respects the due observance of the Sabbath, and yet give no offense to worldly men; for all men have not faith. And how necessary it is that I should be fully persuaded what is duty in my situation, and what is not. There is now a gentleman in the Established Church who was formerly a lieutenant in the royal navy. As he has long been conversant with the sea, and as I consider him a truly pious man, I should be glad to consult his opinion on this subject were I acquainted with him. He is the author of a little work entitled the Retrospect (a work which I have read with much pleasure); and as I have no doubt, reverend sir, you are acquainted with his name, I should be glad you would favor me with it, and also where he resides. I feel a great esteem for him. Would to God I had the same faith, and the same boldness in the cause of Christ, which he manifested while in the navy!

"And now, dear sir, my case is before you, and if you have leisure to make some reflections upon it, and will do me the favor to drop me a few lines by post, I shall feel greatly indebted to you; and though I may never have the pleasure to meet with you on this side eternity, yet my hope is that we shall meet where seas and continents will no longer separate those who belong to the fold of Christ.

"I remain, reverend and dear sir, with Christian affection, yours,

"OBADIAH CONGAR.

"REV. THOS. SCOTT,
"Aston Sandford, Bucks county."

The above letter was forwarded from Liverpool, and the following answer was received in due course of mail:

"Aston Sandford, October 5th, 1817.

"DEAR SIR,—For your very interesting letter induces me thus to address you, though otherwise unknown—you have brought before me a subject which, consulted as I have been in cases of conscience during many years, never before called for my attention, or, indeed, occupied my mind, so that in this respect I am very incompetent to give counsel. I never was at sea, except in the Margate packet to and from London; and never was on board one on the Lord's day, so had no idea in what way the sacred rest might or might not be observed in the management of the vessel. I have been acquainted with pious men who had been commanders of vessels (especially the Rev. Mr. Newton), yet I do not remember to have heard from any of them one word on the subject of your letter.

"Israel was not a seafaring nation, and the case which you state does not appear to be at all alluded to in any regulations of the Mosaic law; and the sailing of the apostles or others, as to long voyages in the New Testament, was generally, if not always, in vessels belonging to the heathen, so that all we can conclude on the subject must be by analogy, and the case resembling or not resembling others concerning which regulations are made or examples recorded; and this shows that there are cases of this kind, in which things are *duties*, for which chapter and verse can not verbatim be quoted, or *sins* which are nowhere in so many words forbidden.

"Arguing, then, from Scriptural principles by analogy, I should first conclude that, by sea as well as land, works of real necessity, of charity, of piety, were no violation of the sacred rest, and thus that every thing was lawful which the safety, or health, or important good, or relief of the persons on board required; this the Lord of the Sabbath, in the New Testament, has fully shown. I should also argue that many things are *necessary* to those under authority which they can not decline, though not so in themselves, as in the case of slaves in the apostles' days in heathen families; to slaves in our West Indies; not to say to servants in many families of Christians, in this land at least.

"In these cases it must often be unavoidable to do as *necessary* to them what is *not necessary* in itself. Your situation as master of the vessel in great measure exempts you and your seamen also from this; but whether regard to the will of your employer (who yet is probably as conceding as most are) may or may not, in some degree, require what otherwise might well be avoided, I must leave you to determine, as well as how far it is practicable or proper for passengers to be made acquainted with your plan in this respect; for if the result be any considerable delay, it will certainly be considered by eager, worldly men as ill usage, and assume in their view the appearance of evil.

"With these previous limitations or cautions, I must, as far as I can judge, reasoning by analogy from Scripture, consider your main principle as well grounded, and your adopting it a proof of a sound judgment, as well as strict conscientiousness. Supposing that the Saturday, and, indeed, all the preceding week, in harvest very unfavorable, and the Lord's day favorable to gathering in the precious grain, though we do not know but the Monday may again be unfavorable, yet sound theologians and conscientious Christians do not think it allowable to violate the sacred rest, and employ the day in harvest work, but to rest on the Sabbath according to the commandment, and trust the Lord as to the future in so doing. Yet in some great emergencies, as, for instance, a bank breaking, and the prospect of an inundation destroying the crop, the necessity might justify an exception in their conduct.

"Thus, then, at sea, whatever relates to the safety of the vessel, &c., must be attended to, as we deem it lawful to fodder our cattle and milk our kine, &c. Emergencies may justify what is somewhat further in several cases, but the main principle seems stable. After even an unfavorable week, the whole advantage of a fair wind must not be taken, if it greatly interfere with the main duties of the sacred rest, but God must be trusted in the path of duty. Yet, perhaps, any thing in altering the sails, so as to forward the voyage, with not more labor than tending the cattle, &c., on land requires, and which can consist with the public and private duties of the day, may be allowable; and it is not desirable to appear stiffly unaccommodating.

"Setting sail on the Lord's day, when it can possibly be avoided, seems altogether wrong, and decidedly to be resisted. In all things we ought to give up our own will to please others for their good, but never give up the Lord's will. Afraid of venturing too far on untrodden ground, I have suggested all the limitations I can recollect. As to the main principle, I can not doubt but in that you are right; yet I fear you should push it too far, and not only be tender in conscience, but uncomfortably scrupulous. May the Lord give you wisdom, and render your example useful to others in your station.

"I am sincerely your friend and servant,

"THOS. SCOTT.

"MR. OBADIAH CONGAR."

CHAPTER IX.

DESPONDENCY CONFESSED, CORRECTED, AND CURED.

THY heart is sad, and deeply thou complain'st
That dull and wandering thy affections prove;
That, lingering far, so often thou remain'st
Apart from Him who claims thy highest love.
Oh, meditate Him more, and the world less:
At morn, and pensive eve, give Him thy thought,
Recall how He hath saved thee, and doth bless
With that redemption, which his life-blood bought:
Then deeply think, till thou hast deeply felt;
When thought is busy, love is busy too.
Oh think, until thy stony heart doth melt,
Of all thy Savior did, and yet will do;
How he hath condescended, suffered, died,
And, even now, doth clasp thee to his bleeding side.

T. C. UPHAM.

WE pass without notice more than two years of the varied sea and shore life of Captain Congar, during which, although there is no evidence of grievous departure from God, religious despondency again stole over him, owing, in part, to a domestic infelicity arising from a want of correspondence of views and feelings on the subject of religion. From August, 1819, onward, there are frequent entries of spiritual exercises and prayers like the following, entitled.

"*A Prayer for Mercy and Peace with God.*

"O God of infinite mercy, who hast said, 'Thou willest not the death of a sinner, but rather that he turn from his ways and live;' and, that backsliders might not be left to despair, hast said, 'Go and proclaim these words toward the north, and say, Return, thou backsliding Israel, saith the Lord, and I will not cause mine anger to fall upon you; for I am merciful, saith the Lord, and I will not keep anger forever. Only acknowledge the iniquity that thou hast transgressed against the Lord thy God.' Now, O Lord, I confess that I am indeed the chief of sinners, and not worthy to lift up my sinful eyes toward thy holy habitation. Yet, O Lord, I deprecate thy wrath; I fear thy frowns; I mourn the hidings of thy face; I am oppressed with anxious forebodings that I shall at last perish from thy presence. Thou, O Lord, seest me filled with melancholy and disconsolate thoughts, and that I spend much of my time in a wretched uncertainty what will be my future destiny.

"I acknowledge, O God, that my sins have hid thy face from me. 'I was shapen in iniquity, and in sin did my mother conceive me.' I confess that, soon as I became capable of moral action, I commenced my sinful career, and as I grew in years I grew in vice. Justly may it be said of me that I drank in iniquity like water. I acknowledge that I have sinned against the pious instructions of a tender and affectionate parent, against the admonitions and convictions of my own conscience, the strivings of thy Holy Spirit, and my most solemn vows and engagements. I have sinned secretly and presumptuously, in thought, word, and deed. I have sinned against mercies and against judgments.

"I confess, O Lord, I have been very rebellious and stiff-necked since the day I was born, that I have walked contrary to thy holy commands, to the dictates of reason, and to my own true interests. I confess that I justly deserve all the distress of mind and all the fears and doubts with which I am afflicted; for too often hast thou called and I refused. Thou hast stretched out thy hand, but I would not regard. Thou mightest now disregard my cry and mock at my fear. O Lord, while I make this mortifying confession, I would mourn that I have sinned against thee. O enable me to repent in dust and ashes. O may this confession produce in my mind an abiding sense of the evil of sin, especially as committed against God, and may I now return to my offended God and Savior, and say, Take away all mine iniquity, and receive me graciously, and do thou heal my backslidings, and love me freely.

"Mercifully sanctify to me the present afflicting state of my mind. O teach me humility and patience, that I may say I will bear the indignation of the Lord, because I have sinned against him. Let me never trust in my own righteousness and strength; but may I look to Jesus alone, who is able to save unto the uttermost. O may I possess unfeigned faith in his blood and righteousness. O divine and heavenly advocate, intercede for me that my faith fail not. O Lord, I beseech thee, have mercy on me, and pardon the numerous transgressions of my life, and restore to me thy favor, which is life, and cause me to walk in the light of thy countenance. Suffer not Satan to tempt me above what I am able to bear. Hear me for the sake of my only high priest and intercessor; and to God the Father, Son, and Holy Ghost be endless praises, Amen."

Thou Man of griefs, remember me,
Who never canst thyself forget,
Thy last mysterious agony,
Thy fainting pangs and bloody sweat.
When, wrestling in the strength of prayer,
Thy spirit sunk beneath its load!
Thy feeble flesh abhorr'd to bear
The wrath of an almighty God!

Father, if I may call thee so,
  Regard my feeble heart's desire;
Remove this load of guilty woe,
  Nor let me in my sins expire
I tremble lest the wrath divine,
  Which bruises now my sinful soul,
Should bruise this wretched soul of mine
  Long as eternal ages roll!
To thee my last distress I bring;
  The heighten'd fear of death I find!
The tyrant, with his direful sting,
  Appears, and hell is close behind!
I deprecate that death alone,
  That endless banishment from thee!
O save, and give me to thy Son,
  Who trembled, wept, and bled for me!

"Throughout this day I have been greatly depressed in spirit, under the apprehension of apostasy from God. We read of the sins of Noah, David, Manasseh, Peter, and Paul, who called himself the chief of sinners; but my sins swell beyond all these. Can there be hope in my case? Yes; a glimmering ray appears through the dark clouds of despairing thoughts which hover over my benighted soul. I hope that the Lord, though greatly offended by my wanderings and backslidings, yet has not totally given me up to impenitency and judicial blindness; I hope the Spirit of grace is not only showing me that my sins have exceeded, but is bringing me to remember my own evil ways, and my doings that were not good, that I might loathe myself in my own sight for my iniquities and for my abominations; I feel that it would be just if God should seal my everlasting destruction, and swear, in his wrath, I shall never enter into his rest. Yet I am a monument of his long-suffering and patience; therefore will I hope in his mercy, and renew my supplications to the throne of grace, that I may be healed of my backslidings, and my soul restored to the image of God, and that I may once more walk in the light of his countenance.

"*A Prayer for the Pardon of Sin and Restoring Grace.*

"O Lord, I beseech thee, look from thy holy habitation in mercy upon thy sinful and polluted creature, who, although beset with fears and doubts, and a deep sense of guilt, would venture to plead with thee, in the name of Jesus, my only hope, that my sins and iniquities may be blotted out from the book of thy remembrance; that I may be healed of all my backslidings; that my sinful soul may be cleansed in that precious blood which cleanseth from all sin; and that the Lord would be pleased to grant me new discoveries of the glories and worthiness of the Divine Redeemer, and his ability to save.

"Dear Savior, thou knowest the strength of my corruption; thou knowest the deceitfulness of my heart; thou knowest the subtlety and power of Satan. O deliver me from my sins and from my fears, and endue me with thy free grace, that I may renounce every beloved idol, and give my heart unto thee. O keep me by thy mighty power through faith unto salvation, and the praise shall be ascribed to the ever-blessed God, Father, Son, and Holy Spirit, world without end. Amen.

"August 24th, 1819, on the way to Oporto. We are surrounded with a multitude of fish which sailors call boneto. They are busily employed catching flying-fish, flocks of which are seen flying every few minutes to escape the jaws of the boneto; but, as they can not fly more than two or three hundred yards at a time, the dolphin and boneto keep so near under them, that as soon as they light in the water they become a prey. The Psalmist says, 'These all wait upon thee, that thou mayest give them their meat in due season; that thou givest them they gather; thou openest thine hand, they are filled with good.' This kind of fish are rather scarce on the ocean, and in general are difficult to take; yet, extraordinary as it is, they have followed the ship more than three weeks, and we find no difficulty in taking them at any time. They are not generally held to be very palatable, notwithstanding they make a pretty good mess, by way of a change.

"The sea is smooth, the sky serene, and gentle breezes are wafting our ship along the briny way in stately magnificence, with all her canvas spread. Our crew are all in good health. The principal part of our little company attend religious worship morning and evening, and in a very becoming manner, and I hope to some profit. I have myself enjoyed a great share of health this voyage, and we have had a large proportion of fine, comfortable weather.

"But, with all these favors, there is one thing to remind me that this is not the place of my rest. The enjoyment of His presence who has created all these things is wanted. This day, indeed, I trust the Lord has condescended to speak in some degree comfortably to my troubled mind. I feel a hope that the Spirit of grace has not utterly forsaken me. The gracious condescension of Jehovah, and his promises of mercy to the idolatrous and disobedient Jews, which we find in the sixteenth chapter of Ezekiel, from the sixtieth verse to the end, and again, from the twenty-first verse of the thirty-sixth chapter to the end, encourages me to hope that the Lord will yet be favorable to me, but not for my sake. Yet, though the Lord has been pleased to make known his purposes of mercy even to those who have been very rebellious for his own name's sake, he still says he will be inquired of by the house of Israel to do those things for them. O may I now with a holy importunity beseech the Father of mercies to cast an eye of pity toward his helpless creature, and may my cries, sprinkled with the atoning blood of Jesus, reach his mercy-seat and receive a gracious answer.

"*A Prayer with Thanksgiving for some Gracious Tokens of Divine Favor.*

"O Lord God! I acknowledge that I am less than the least of all thy mercies. I have forfeited every right to thy compassions. I have strayed from thee like a lost sheep. I confess that my sins have provoked thee to withdraw from me thy wonted favor. Thou, O God! hast justly hedged up my way, and made my paths crooked. Yet I thank thee, O thou God of mercy! that a ray of hope is still afforded me under the darkness of my mind and the hidings of thy face. I thank thee that I am permitted to indulge the consoling reflection that there is forgiveness with thee, that thou mayest be feared. I pray, O Lord, that the necessities of my case may plead for my importunity, and that thou wouldst verify thy promises of faithfulness and truth wherein thou hast caused me to hope, and carry on thy begun goodness to me, O Lord, until I can say with thy servant of old, 'Lord, thou knowest all things, thou knowest I love thee.' Will the Lord hear my prayer and attend unto my cry for his own holy name's sake, and to the only wise God, Father, Son, and Spirit, I would render everlasting praises, Amen.

"Thursday, 26th. I begin to feel more and more sensible that my case, as it respects my spiritual condition, calls for extraordinary thoughtfulness and solemnity, and, if there be any remedy, to apply to it with all that solicitude and diligence which my peculiar situation requires. In looking over my journal, I find that about eleven years since I was much oppressed with doubts and fears, and that, after laboring under these difficulties of mind for some time, I resolved to seek unto God, by fasting and prayer, for relief. The Lord was gracious to me, and delivered me from all my fears and apprehensions. Am I not, then, encouraged to look to Him in the same way for the removal of present anxieties, and that he would once more set my soul at liberty from the bondage of death and sin, and cause me to rejoice in his salvation?

"But it is not by past experience only that I feel encouraged to hope and wait on the Lord by renewed importunity for a favorable change, but by the solemn exhortations and promises of the Lord himself; for he says, in the second chapter of Joel and twelfth verse, 'Therefore also now, saith the Lord, turn ye even to me with all your heart, and with fasting, and with weeping, and with mourning; and rend your heart, and not your garments, and turn unto the Lord your God: for he is gracious and merciful, slow to anger, and of great kindness, and repenteth him of the evil. Who knoweth if he will return and repent, and leave a blessing behind him; even a meat-offering and a drink-offering, unto the Lord your God.' And again, in the sixth chapter of Matthew and at the seventeenth verse, our Savior teaches not only how to fast acceptably, but promises important blessings in answer to the performance of this duty.

"Hoping in the mercy and faithfulness of God, I resolve, by the assistance of his grace, to seek unto him more earnestly, until he be pleased to appoint unto me beauty for ashes, the oil of joy for mourning, and the garment of praise for the spirit of heaviness. And oh! may

I experience all this mercy for his own name's sake.

"From this time onward the remainder of our passage, my mind was more than usually occupied with reflecting on the sins of my life, and endeavoring to humble myself before God on account thereof; and I felt as though nothing could give me enjoyment unless I once more experienced some tokens of the Lord's gracious designs toward me. I did not long continue in that state of fearful apprehension that the mercy of God was clean gone, and that I should never again enjoy his favor; for I began to entertain a feeble hope that my case was not irrecoverable, and this hope excited me to plead more earnestly for the forgiveness of all my sins, and that through grace I might make a new surrender of myself unto God, to be his for time and eternity, resolving henceforth to be more watchful over my heart and life, that I might not sin against God or bring a disgrace on religion.

"On the twentieth of September came on a most violent gale of wind, which continued almost incessantly for three days. The good hand of God was displayed in a striking manner in preserving us from the perils which surrounded us, and which threatened our safety. To Him only who holds the winds in his fists could we look in the time of our trouble, and, blessed be his name, he not only rebuked the sea, and granted us moderate weather, but sent us favorable winds, and conducted us safely into our desired port. On the next Sabbath I was favored with an opportunity of going to the house of God, and offering up my thanksgiving, and paying my vows. And O, blessed be the name of the Most High, who hath not only restored me to my home and to the society of my family and friends, but hath granted me once more, I trust, some discoveries of his love and mercy to my soul; hath banished, in a great degree, my doubts and fears, so that I am enabled to rejoice in the light of his countenance. I do feel as though this promise was verified to me, 'I will cast thine iniquities into the depths of the sea, and remember them no more.'

"But oh, why all this condescension to me, the chief of sinners? I can only say, even so, Father, for so it seemeth good in thy sight. I would be thankful for all those Divine rebukes and corrections which have been the means of humbling me under his mighty hand; and it is my prayer, if I be not deceived, that whatever methods the Lord may see fit to use with me, I might always be kept, not only humble for my sins which are past, but sensible, also, of my entire dependence on the grace of the Lord Jesus to assist me in resisting sin and temptation for the time to come."

What may be my future lot,
Well I know concerns me not;
This should set my heart at rest,
What thy will ordains is best.
I my all to thee resign:
Father, let my will be thine;
May but all thy dealings prove
Fruits of thy paternal love.
Guard me, Savior, by thy power,
Guard me in the trying hour;
Let thy unremitted care
Save me from the lurking snare.
Let my few remaining days
Be directed to thy praise;
So the last, the closing scene,
Shall be tranquil and serene.
To thy will I leave the rest,
Grant me but this one request:
Both in life and death to prove
Tokens of thy special love.

Chapter X.

ABANDONMENT OF THE SEA. TRAVELS AND EXPERIENCE IN THE SOUTHWEST.

What matter whether pain or pleasures fill
  The swelling heart one little moment here?
From both alike how vain is every thrill,
  While an untried eternity is near!
Think not of rest, fond man, in life's career,
  The joys and griefs that meet thee, dash aside
Like bubbles, and thy bark right onward steer,
  Through calm and tempest, till it cross the tide,
  Shoot into port in triumph, or serenely glide.

Carlos Wilcox

Being now upward of fifty years of age, and having acquired a patrimony sufficient, in his judgment, to carry him along for some years, Captain Congar resolved upon quitting the sea, and undertaking something else for a livelihood and employment. This, had he purchased a spot of ground and turned to farming, would have been judicious, and there is good reason to believe would have succeeded well, as it often does with men in his line of life. But finding himself and wife unable to agree as to the course to be pursued, and seeing their difference of opinion was one that could not be easily settled, and was likely, he thought, to lead to serious difficulties, he drew the conclusion that it would be useless for him to attempt any kind of business at home, and that the best way was to endeavor to effect some business arrangement abroad.

In one view, after the example of the prudent man, who foreseeth the evil and hideth himself, this was wise as it was bold; but, in the large view of things, it would have been far better for him to have resumed his business on the deep. Having taken his resolution to banish himself a while from his family and friends,

> The world was all before him, where to choose
> His place of rest, and Providence his guide.

"My great desire," he says, "was that I might not be banished from God's presence, and that wherever I might be directed to sojourn, I might be useful, and be prepared for his holy dispensations. From the time my thoughts were first turned to this business, I earnestly besought the Lord to direct me in all my steps, to open a way in his providence to follow some useful occupation, and that I might see the path of duty clear in all things. It was, indeed, an affecting thought to leave my native town, where I had enjoyed much in the society of connections and friends—where the Gospel was preached in its purity, and where so many interesting scenes had taken place—to sojourn I knew not whither, and perhaps never to see the face of those I love again in the land of the living. But what is this world? What can it give? Alas! it only brings cares and anxieties, and happy is he who, delivered from its troubles, has reached the haven of rest above."

On the thirteenth of November, 1820, he took passage to New Orleans with a small assortment of goods, and thence to Natchez, where he arrived on the thirteenth of December, busying himself at all stopping-places with distributing tracts. Landing there a stranger, he seems to have expected little else than troubles. But, after landing his goods and getting them stored, he called on an old acquaintance, the Reverend William Woodbridge, who gave him much useful information relative to the place, and also introduced him to respectable friends. "From him," says the Journal, "I learned that the state of religion was melancholily low, that very few followers of Jesus were to be found, and that vice and iniquity greatly abounded. This was, indeed, a sad reflection to me; but it has been the subject of my prayers, from first to last, that I might be directed where to sojourn, and this would appear to be the spot. I can not, indeed, calculate, should I remain here, on any thing but trials. But may the good hand of God preserve me from sin and temptation, and give me some good to do at this place.

"I must not omit to notice, and I would do it with humble gratitude to Almighty God for rendering my whole journey to this place so comfortable and prosperous, that, had I been delayed only three days longer on my way, the consequences might have been highly disastrous. My goods were landed and put in store on the thirteenth. On the evening of Friday, the fifteenth, came on a tremendous storm of lightning and thunder, with torrents of rain. So violent were the shocks of thunder, the house shook to the very foundation, and the windows rattled as though they would have fled from their places. I slept that night alone at Mr. Woodbridge's, but I never knew what it was to enjoy a calm and serene frame of mind in such an awful scene before. I laid me down while the earth comparatively shook under me, and went to sleep. The Sabbath night following the same scene took place, and until this time, Tuesday, it is still raining, and continues bad traveling; consequently, had I reached here at this time, my goods would have been liable to injury and loss, and to great expense in securing them. After having made every inquiry and searched through the town to procure a store, or part of a store, I at length agreed with Messrs. Berthe & Co. to take their old stand, and to pay forty dollars a month for six months.

"On Friday, the 22d, I commenced opening, and on Saturday made some good sales. Among the many instances of Divine goodness which I have been the subject of since I left home, I would not forget to record the gracious condescension and love of God in granting me some precious manifestations of his presence and favor. He has spoken peace to my soul, and restored to me the joy of his salvation. And why is all this favor shown to me, the most unworthy of the race of Adam? For his name's sake he declares in the thirty-second verse of the thirty-sixth chapter of Ezekiel, 'Not for your sakes do I do this, saith the Lord God, be it known unto you: be ashamed and confounded for your own ways, O house of Israel.'

"The first and second month after I commenced business at Natchez, I sold quite as much as I had any reason to expect, whereat I was encouraged to send to New Orleans for a supply of such articles as were wanted to keep my assortment good. In order to be at as little expense as possible, and that I might not be absent from my shop, I lived alone at my place of business, and often felt keenly the want of society. Yet even in solitude I found pleasures which a busy world does not meddle with. My greatest anxieties were always excited by reflecting on the future course which it would be best to pursue. To spend my days here in solitude, even if I were successful in business, seemed a melancholy thought."

By the end of February, 1821, business had fallen off, and a letter received at the same time from his wife, bewailing his absence and begging his return, wrought in him commiseration.

> Soon his heart relented
> Toward her, his life so late and sole delight,
> Now at his feet submissive in distress.

"My prayers," he says, "were now more earnestly lifted to the Supreme Governor of the universe that I might be directed whither to remove; and trusting in the promise annexed to the command to 'commit thy way unto the Lord,' I endeavored to wait until some providence might point the path I ought to pursue.

"While my mind was thus occupied from day to day, I received a second letter from my wife, in which she again mentioned her low estate of health, and especially that her spirits were greatly depressed. After perusing her letter, the relation she gave of her difficulties and trials so affected my mind that I could no longer hesitate what to do. I resolved to make the most of my goods as soon as possible, and, if spared, to return home, leaving all my affairs in the hands of Him who gave me my being." Having procured a release from his obligations in respect to the store occupied by him, he made immediate arrangements for leaving and returning North.

"And now," he writes, "I desire to acknowledge the goodness of God toward me since I left home. I have enjoyed a good degree of health; I have been protected from many surrounding evils; I have been prospered in my business in a measure equal to my expectations; I have found some pleasant and Christian society; I have enjoyed great privileges in this place; and especially would I make mention of the loving-kindness of the Lord in granting me, I trust, some precious tokens of his favor, and in his purposes of everlasting mercy to my soul. And while I confess much imperfection and many failures in duty, I would record with gratitude what the Lord has done for me. 'Oh! my soul, bless the Lord; show forth his salvation from day to day.'"

On his return to the north, by way of New Orleans, he was brought very low with the dysentery common upon the Mississippi, and, in prospect of dying, his soul was flooded with peace. His life, however, was spared, and he reached his family convalescent by way of the sea. Nothing better opening in a business way at Newark during the summer, he embarked in the fall again for Natchez, with his family, consisting of his wife and her sister. His business adventure was successful, and, the proceeds thereof being invested in cotton, they returned to the North in the summer of 1822. This expedition, dangerous as it then was from pirates by sea and yellow fever in port, was repeated for two or three successive seasons.

In November, when just arrived at Natchez, through many perils, we find him recording with gratitude, in view of the gracious providences that had appeared in his behalf, "Verily I can say the Lord is my shade on my right hand, therefore I have not been greatly moved. I would also remember the goodness of God in sparing my wife, and affording her so much health. Our fears at leaving New York, lest some person on board might have the yellow fever, were great; and no less so were they lest some of us might take the disease in New Orleans. We have had a large share of health, and have been delivered from all those evils which, for the time, produced some degree of terror; and no less were our fears of falling into the hands of pirates, than of falling a prey to the malignant diseases which banished many of the citizens of New York and New Orleans from their homes. May we be enabled at all times to cherish a due sense of our obligations to the God of our lives, whose mercies, indeed, are more than can be reckoned up."

His speculations and ventures in 1823 did not turn out as advantageously as they had done; and this, there is reason to believe, worrying the wife more than the husband, elicited in his journal the following sensible considerations upon a practical matter, the truth and the applicability of which to many cases, rather than any peculiar originality or profoundness, justify their insertion here: "There is a subject which sometimes is talked of among professors of religion, and appears to them of vast importance, which yet, notwithstanding, when human passions get the ascendency, loses all its weight and influence on the mind, and is forgotten. I allude to the practice of Christians marrying with unbelievers. In the 6th chapter of 2d Corinthians, 14th verse and onward, this practice is expressly prohibited by the apostle as utterly inconsistent; 'For,' says he, 'what fellowship hath righteousness with unrighteousness? and what communion hath light with darkness?' &c., as if he had said, 'Two can not walk together except they be agreed. There can be no union of heart where two diametrically opposite principles govern; and where there is no union of heart and principles, there can be no concord.'

"It is strange that where so much is at stake there should frequently be discoverable so great an unwillingness to let the judgment rule instead of the passions. Through this error thousands have plunged themselves into all the miseries of a guilty conscience, and the mortifying reflection that they have entered into league and covenant with an enemy of God. I am inclined to believe that few Christians have ever committed this error without repenting of it all the days of their lives after. Scarcely a day will pass without some transaction taking place which will cause grief and solicitude on the part of the one who would conscientiously walk in the ways of God's holy commands.

"The Christian sees every object in a different light from the unregenerate person. The

Christian's God is the Lord of heaven and earth; the unregenerate person's god is this world with its vanities. The Christian's end and aim is to do something for the advancement of the Redeemer's kingdom among men; the unregenerate person's end is to advance self, to increase wealth, to live in luxury and ease. The Christian feels it obligatory to devote a part of every day to secret prayer, and to contribute a portion of his worldly substance, as God hath prospered, to benevolent objects; the unregenerate person's language is, what need of so much solicitude about religion—we have need of all we can earn for our own use, for we know not what shall befall us, and we ought to provide for a rainy day, and so on.

"A Christian friend must not be introduced into the family, lest the subject of religion becomes the topic of conversation, and the thoughts of religion always produce uneasiness in the mind of the unregenerate. On the other hand, gay, vain, and foolish company never can suit the mind that is looking beyond this terrestrial ball for something more substantial and lasting.

"There will therefore exist a constant *source of disquietude and perturbation*, which nothing can dispel but Almighty grace. How dangerous is it for Christians to marry with unbelievers: how unhappy it is sure to make them! The Christian can not engage in any benevolent enterprise, but the unregenerate clog is always hanging back; or, if it go, it must be carried, for it has no feet to walk, no eyes to see, no tongue to talk."

Notwithstanding the peculiar trials of Captain Congar, and his unfavorable changing life, there is evidence in these years of a pretty uniform growth in grace, and an abiding fixedness of purpose to glorify and serve God. In a subsequent passage South to that referred to above, after enumerating the Divine providential favors to himself and family, he adds, with great appearance of sincerity and fervor, "But the greatest of all blessings bestowed upon the chief of sinners is in general (if I be not deceived, and I trust I am not, by the spirit which he hath given me) a uniform and comfortable hope that I am interested in the covenant mercy of God through Jesus Christ; that he has wrought in my soul a work of grace, which is an earnest of the complete perfection of soul and body in his heavenly kingdom; and, having such hopes, I endeavor, in some measure, to purify myself as Christ is pure. But, alas, my sin and folly! Not a day of my life but I am called upon to lament more or less misspent time, some thought, word, or deed which is contrary to the Divine requirements, and inconsistent with my own most solemn vows and engagements. When will the time come that I shall love the Lord with all my heart, and my neighbor as myself? May the Lord create in me a new heart, and renew a right spirit within me.

"Wednesday, twenty-ninth of October. The winds are favorable, but very light. At eight o'clock A.M. made the land, being what is called the Harbor Islands. We are all well on board, in number about forty persons besides myself; and, alas! what a melancholy reflection, that I find no good grounds to believe there is *one truly pious individual among them!* It might, indeed, be thought, that in the judgment of that charity which believeth all things, which hopeth all things, I ought to form a different conclusion, and not discover so much partiality or selfishness as to think unfavorably of every one but myself.

"There is no doubt but self-preference is interwoven with our very natures, so that a mixture of it may be seen even in those who are most distinguished for their graces. But in forming our opinion relative to the state and condition of our fellow-men in a religious point of view, we must always be governed by the decision of the Bible, and therefore what the Bible approves we must approve, and what the Bible condemns we must condemn.

"When, therefore, we see men from day to day spending their whole time playing cards, frequently taking their Maker's name in vain, and idling away the Sabbath, or vainly amusing themselves by reading some novel or trifling publication, while the Bible is wholly neglected, what can we say? Must we not conclude there is no fear of God before their eyes? And surely there can be no love of God in their hearts.

"Here, then, some might suppose is a great opening to do good, an opportunity to suggest occasionally the great concerns of the soul, and seeking the knowledge of God; yet, in general, the fear of souring the minds of those around me by introducing a subject to which the human heart is so much averse, together with a want of capacity for discussing even those things which, to my own apprehension, are perfectly clear and satisfactory, hinders me from doing much save distributing a few tracts. With what feelings, then, should I indulge the hope, that while so many are left in nature's darkness, and living daily without any due sense of the evil of sin, and regardless of the way of escape from the wrath to come, I alone, who am the chief of sinners, should be made a monument of Divine mercy! Surely the ways of the Lord are not as our ways, neither his thoughts like our thoughts. I pray that I may never lose sight of my original state by nature, nor of the exceeding wickedness of my former practices, nor yet my manifold imperfections and shortcomings, lest, being lifted up with spiritual pride, I should think myself to be something when I am nothing.

"Friday, 31st. Passing the Berry Islands, with a pleasant breeze and delightful weather. I never come this way without noticing how exactly the temperature of this climate suits my habit and constitution, and I often wish these islands were fertile and inhabited, that I might find an abode where the cold winds of the north could not reach me, and where the summer heat would not relax the system as it does in the southern sections of my own country. But why should I make calculations, or imagine that this or that country, or place, or society would afford those pleasures which are unfading, durable, and pure?"

His experience found itself portrayed in the lines of Madam Guyon:

Thou, Lord, alone, art all thy children need,
  And there is none beside:
From thee the streams of blessedness proceed;
  In thee the bless'd abide.
Fountain of life and all-abounding grace,
Our source, our center, and our dwelling place.

With me remains nor place nor time,
  My country is in every clime:
I can be safe and free from care
  On every shore, for God is there.

"But ah! the thought that my wife is still in the gall of bitterness and bond of iniquity often makes me go mourning all the day long. When I reflect on her situation as a sinner, and apparently becoming more and more insensible of her sad state, and when I find, also, her unwillingness to converse on the subject of religion, and, at the same time, fear she indulges some kind of a false hope, I feel under serious apprehensions for her eternal welfare, and cease not to pray for her, although, I may add, with a feeble hope. But I endeavor still to commend her to the mercy of God, who is a wise and holy sovereign, and who has a right to do with his creatures as seemeth good in his sight. I beseech the Lord, for Christ's sake, to give me grace to pray for her more fervently, and from pure and holy motives, that his name may be glorified in her salvation. O Lord, let her not perish through my sin and unfaithfulness. Saturday, first of November. Light winds and very unpleasant weather: sailing over the Banks all the past night and this day, in three fathoms water. The thermometer is generally about seventy-eight degrees—to-day it stands at eighty-one degrees; but, notwithstanding the weather is warm, it is by no means oppressive. At three P. M., it being nearly calm, and not wishing to go off the Banks with so light a wind, we came to anchor in ten fathoms water.

"We continued at anchor until the day following, when, at two P. M., a smart breeze suddenly sprung up from the northward and eastward, which we readily embraced by getting under way and standing on our course. We steered west-southwest, going eight miles per hour. At two o'clock in the morning the watch on deck supposed they saw breakers ahead, which, for the instant, threw us in the utmost confusion. The ship was immediately wore round, and brought under snug sail until morning. Then, having discovered the Double-headed-shot Keys as far as we could see to the eastward, we concluded that our fears had been groundless. Tried the temperature of the water, and found it seventy-eight degrees, and the air, in the shade, seventy-four. Thursday,

6th. The wind continued favorable: at two P.M., saw the land about the Balize bearing west three leagues.

"Sabbath, 9th. The holy Scriptures declare this is the day the Lord hath made. But, alas! how little is it regarded by many on ship or shore; and what numerous occasions does the water-business give men for profaning the Lord's day by working thereupon, without exposing them to the censures of the godly and Sabbath-keeping. But they forget that the Sabbath's avenging Lord is eyeing them, and is sure to bring them up:

"'Who resteth not one day in seven,
That soul shall never rest in heaven.'

My soul is grieved at seeing all hands on board, with about twenty slaves besides, employed in warping the ship through the English Turn, with the wind ahead—a thing for which none can plead the least pretense of necessity.

"I can not help remarking the power of unbelief in the carnal heart, and the determination which it manifests to reject every thing which does not accord with its own notion. A striking instance of this I have noticed in the conduct and conversation of our captain. He seems willing to allow that the Scriptures contain many things which are excellent, and well calculated to promote the good of mankind, but by no means acknowledges that the whole of it is the word of God, and absolutely considers some part of it too horrible ever to have been published; and yet allows that those who live strictly according to its requirements will eventually have the advantage of all others, but says he wishes he had never read it.

"Respecting his conclusions relative to the Bible, he is confirmed in his opinion by observing that many of those who profess to believe its authenticity, and to take it for their rule and guide, do not appear to be better men than others, nor is it discoverable that they are influenced by purer principles. Would to God these remarks did not apply to myself. I blush and am ashamed to think how often I have occasioned a reproach to religion. O Lord, cleanse me from secret faults, and keep back thy servant from presumptuous sins; let them not have the dominion over me. Through thy grace I will endeavor to be more consistent."

Jehovah, sov'reign of my heart!
My joy by night and day!
From thee, oh! never more I'll part,
From thee ne'er go astray.

Whene'er allurements round me stand
  And tempt me from my choice,
Oh! let me find thy gracious hand;
  Oh! let me hear thy voice.
This vain and feeble heart, I know,
  To worldly ways is prone;
But penitential tears shall show
  There's joy in thee alone.
With God all darkness turns to day;
  With him all sorrows flee;
Thou art the true and living way,
  And I will walk in thee.

Chapter XI.

BUSINESS, BENEVOLENCE, AND MENTAL EXERCISES ON SHORE CONTINUED.

Thus, lady, fares the man that hath prepared
A Rest for his desires; and sees all things
Beneath him; and hath learned this Book of Man,
Full of the notes of frailty; and compared
The best of glory with her sufferings:
By whom I see you labor all you can
To plant your heart, and set your thoughts as near
His glorious Mansion as your powers can bear.

Old Daniel.

Up to the year 1828 Captain Congar continued to spend his winters in Natchez, doing business successfully with the assortments of goods which he brought with him from the North from year to year. He engaged zealously in the Sabbath school and the support of religious ordinances in the Southwest, and was much esteemed by a circle of Christian friends as a man of high integrity, conscientiousness, and religious zeal. He records frequently, with devout gratitude, his providential deliverances by sea and land in going to and fro, sometimes on the floating steam volcanoes of the Mississippi and other waters of the West, sometimes in the dangerous navigation of the Capes of Florida.

The malignant diseases of the climate, as the bilious, yellow, and coast fevers, he was happily preserved from; but both himself and wife had occasional attacks of the fever and ague, which few at that time escaped. During an illness of his wife at Natchez in 1826, his affection as a tender husband and Christian was sorely tried. "How," said he, "did my bowels yearn over her, when, in an agony of pain, she would cry for mercy! Her distress, during these paroxysms, has torn my very heart with grief and dismay. Oh! that she might indeed find mercy for the sake of Jesus Christ, who hath opened a door of mercy through his atoning blood, even for those who, sensible of their misery, come to him at the eleventh hour. Although I felt unwilling to leave her for a moment, yet I was constrained to retire for a little when an opportunity offered, to plead at the throne of grace on her behalf. I wrestled in her behalf that this sore trial might be sanctified to her, and be made the means of bringing her to see that she needed salvation from sin as well as from suffering. Through the Divine goodness, she was soon restored to usual health again."

In the summer of 1829 we find him established in business at Savannah, Georgia, and this is a fragment of his autobiography on entering upon his sixty-second year: "June 27th, 1829. I have now the satisfaction to record the goodness of Almighty God to me in the numerous instances of his kindness through every period of my existence, and particularly for permitting me to enter upon the sixty-second year of my age in so much health, enjoying the use of my reason, surrounded with friends, and especially favored with a comfortable hope that my sins are pardoned and my name written in heaven, through the boundless mercy of God in Christ Jesus, to whom be glory forever, Amen. I have, indeed, great reason to be humbled for my sins of the year past, as well as of my whole life. May I henceforth redeem my misspent time, and weave more carefully my warp of life, since its threads must be nearly through. Many things are admonishing me of life's uncertainty. Day before yesterday this city was visited with a destructive storm of lightning and rain. The thunderbolts were in such swift and startling succession that men thought the artillery of the last day was discharging upon them, and that the advance couriers of the judgment had come. A woman and her child, about four years of age, were killed instantly. A horse was also killed, a vessel's mast shivered, and a house struck. Verily, in the midst of life we are in death. Oh! may my future days, be they many or few, be devoted to the service of my God and Savior, that when death comes, whether suddenly or with long warning, I may have nothing to do but die."

In the winter of 1830, his business being depressed, and being afflicted also with sore sickness in his family, he seems to have fallen again into a state of painful despondency. Remembering that as iron sharpeneth iron, so doth the countenance of a man his friend, he wisely called upon two of the elders of the Church, and freely communicated with them respecting his spiritual concerns. They treated him, he says, with great kindness and skill, and prayed with him, and from this time forward his mind was much relieved, and was enabled in a measure, as before, to rejoice in the Lord. But the situation of his wife, both as to her bodily and spiritual estate, excited his deepest solicitude.

In April we find him saying, "It is with a degree of heartfelt gratitude to Almighty God that I am enabled once more to cherish a comfortable hope that I have found mercy and grace in his sight. I am still, indeed, oppressed with a deep sense of sin and of the awful depravity of the human heart, but I am freed in a good degree from that dark, despairing frame of mind which seemed almost to overwhelm me at times. I trust God is faithful. Jesus Christ is the same yesterday, to-day, and forever. I hope I have committed my cause to him, and that he hath heard my prayers; and I think I feel thankful for those chastisements which have been the means of bringing me to consider my ways and doings, which were not good.

"I have found the exercises and solemnities of the communion season well suited to relieve the mind of the doubting and desponding sinner who still hopes the Lord has not utterly forsaken him, who still hopes the Spirit of grace is exciting him to a more firm and uniform reliance on the mercy of God in Christ for every blessing, and waiting and longing for new and brighter discoveries of the Divine perfections, and for a more complete deliverance from the bondage of sin. I think I can say in truth that, in general, from the communion season until this day, I have experienced some sweet tokens of the Lord's kindness.

"Tuesday, August 24th. This day has been

recommended by our pastor to be observed as a day of fasting, humiliation, and prayer, that God would revive the languishing graces of his own people, and stir them up to a greater concern for his glory and the salvation of souls. At ten A.M. a goodly number met, and the exercises were interesting, and such as were calculated to arouse the slumbering Christian and bring the unhumbled sinner to feel his danger. As regards myself, my mind for some days past has been more than ordinarily employed with serious thoughts relative to my own spiritual condition. Methinks I have seen more and more of the deceitfulness of my heart than ever, and I do groan, being burdened. I fear I have thought myself to be something when I was nothing. I am resolved, by Divine assistance, to watch my heart and life with more care, and to make it my business to compare, not only my outward conduct, but the temple of my heart, with the requirements of the Gospel, and to bring all my thoughts and actions to that test. I feel resolved to engage in good earnest in a holy warfare with the powers of darkness, and not to spare my own lusts and corruptions, but seek to have them all slain through the power of the great Captain of my salvation. Satan, I know, will roar and fling his fiery darts. Dear Savior, shield me, and grant me deliverance, that I may yet sing a song of victory, and praise thy name for thy loving kindness and for thy truth."

Oh! that I had not this divided heart,
A mind self-sunder'd, and at war within;
Which gives, or seems to give, to Heaven a part,
But gives, alas! a greater part to sin.
Sometimes I think the victory to gain,
And plant my standard on the heavenly height;
But suddenly imperious passions reign,
And put my faithfulness and hopes to flight.
My conscience prompts me to the better way,
The Holy Spirit makes it still more clear;
But foul temptation leads my steps astray,
And heaven is lost, because the world is dear.
'Tis he in triumph and in peace shall run
The Christian's trying race, whose heart, whose soul is one.

His business adventures not succeeding in Savannah so prosperously as they had hoped for, and restlessness in his family consequent, probably in great degree, upon ill health calling for a change, Captain Congar removed in 1831 to St. Augustine, East Florida, not, he said, that it offered much as a place of business, but as a climate more congenial to their habits and constitutions than any other in the United States. He purchased a small homestead and store there, with the design of a permanent abode for the remainder of his days; and he engaged in humble religious labors, in connection with the Presbyterian Church, with his wonted zeal and conscientiousness, obtaining, in a high degree, the confidence of the whole community, and the warm regard of a circle of friends.

But in the year 1838, a settled dissatisfaction in his family, arising, in part, from an interruption of friendly intercourse with the directors of the St. Augustine Banking Institution, and more, perhaps, from internal unrest and disquiet, compelled him, though sorely against his will, to transfer his residence first to St. Mary's, Georgia, and thence to Jacksonville, Florida, meanwhile visiting at the North. His desire to do good and to glorify God held him fast through changes that were far from satisfactory or profitable to one in his years.

On his seventieth birth-day, June 27th, 1838, being on a visit to Newark, surveying the mercies of his active and green old age, and looking beyond the cloud that just then hung over him, we find him thus resolving, as in the vigor of youth: "To use the world as not abusing it, renouncing it as his portion, and keeping it under foot; to resist the powers of darkness, and to live to the glory of God. It is, indeed, but little I can expect to do the remainder of my days, either for God my Maker, Christ my Redeemer, or my fellow-man. I consider my days of activity and usefulness, if, indeed, I have ever been useful, nearly at an end. But I beseech the Most High to succor and strengthen me to do his will, and to enable me to bear up under the trials, vicissitudes, and changes of this mortal life without complaining, trusting in his name that all will be well.

"We remained in New York and among our friends until the beginning of September following. After much deliberation and prayer, it was finally agreed upon by us both that it would be best to return to Florida as soon as convenient, and with a view to locate ourselves at Jacksonville (a new place), about twenty miles from the St. John's Bar."

Having purchased a new stock of goods with this view, they took passage in the schooner Essex, Captain Jeffery. Just after leaving New York they experienced a heavy gale of wind, and lost both anchors; but, having obtained a pilot, they were successful in running the vessel upon the beach, without loss of life. The wind afterward subsiding, the vessel was lightened, got off, and taken to the city for repairs.

On the thirtieth day of September they embarked again, and, after a pleasant passage of nine days, arrived safe over the St. John's Bar. Reaching Jacksonville on the twelfth of October, he says, "We engaged a house, landed our goods, and commenced business immediately. Thus far the Lord has led me on. Thus far his power prolongs my days."

Here Captain Congar was permitted to spend a period of seven years, respected, beloved, and useful, up to that immediately preceding the date of his death. On the anniversary of his seventy-third birth-day there is this entry: "My earthly race is well-nigh run. I shall have little more to do with a world in arms against its Sovereign, the great and mighty God. With that Sovereign I have an advocate, even Jesus Christ the righteous, and he is the propitiation for my sins. O blessed Advocate, plead my cause, do all for me, and strengthen me to do and to suffer all thou wilt appoint me; and all the days of my appointed time let me wait till my change come, and be more consistent than I have been as a member of the community, as the head of a family, and as a professed follower of the Lamb.

"It was the Psalmist's saying, 'One thing have I desired, that will I seek after.' This do I pant after with my whole heart, to be emptied of self and the world, and filled, like a vacant vessel, with all the fullness of God. The world is dead to me, and I am dead to the world, though still busy in it. Its maxims, its fashions, its amusements, its pleasures, its acquisitions, how gladly I can quit them all."

World, adieu, thou real cheat,
  Oft have thy deceitful charms
Fill'd my heart with fond conceit,
  Foolish hopes and false alarms:
Now I see as clear as day
How thy follies pass away.

Vain thy entertaining sights;
  False thy promises renew'd;
All the pomp of thy delights
  Does but flatter and delude:
Thee I quit for heaven above,
Object of the noblest love.

"Could I be sure that my days of usefulness were at an end which my heavenly Father appoints to me, I think I could have done with all terrestrial things without one sigh but that I had not better served my Lord and Master. The hopes which religion inspires are now my only solace in the worldly work which I have still to do. The cares and business of this life only harass and vex; the consolations of religion calm and soothe. Oh! that the longer I dwell here, the more I may become transformed into the image of my Savior; that, when death comes, I may doff all mortal fear, and shout in triumph, through Him who makes me conquer, 'O Death, where is thy sting! O Grave, where is thy victory!'"

SOMETIMES I upward lift mine eyes,
  And, fill'd with pleasure, see
The happy hosts that throng the skies,
  The blood-wash'd company.
How beautiful their robes, I say;
  Their garments all, how white!
Fair as the sun's ascending ray,
  And clear as noon-day light.

Oh Savior, thou hast made them clean,
  The garments they do wear;
And all who wash in thee their sin,
  May in those garments share.
Let me, too, wear that spotless dress,
  Its beauty may I prove:
That robe of finish'd holiness,
  The garb of perfect love!

CHAPTER XII.

LIFE, LABORS, AND EXPERIENCE AT JACKSONVILLE.

THAT man may last, but never lives,
Who much receives, but nothing gives;
Whom none can love, whom none can thank,
Creation's blot, creation's blank.
But he who marks, from day to day,
In generous acts his radiant way,
Treads the same path his Savior trod,
The path to glory and to God.—GIBBONS.

IN accordance with his usual energy and zeal in the things of religion, Captain Congar had not been long in Jacksonville before we find him earnestly engaged in measures for its moral and spiritual improvement. His record of events and of personal observations and doings there is not so full as in years before, but something is supplied by letters to friends.

In a communication to a sister in Newark, dated Jacksonville, East Florida, August 15th, 1842, he says: "I have several subjects which call my attention in writing you at this time, and which I might touch upon a little; but it is sometimes with me as it is with some preachers I have heard, who, having arranged their intended discourse under several heads, commence thus: 'In the first place, let me call your attention to the consideration of the first clause of such a verse;' after which they forget to say any thing about the second, third, or fourth place, and go on promiscuously. But on this occasion I say, in the first place, Mary and myself have both been highly favored with usual health; not that we are altogether without the infirmities of human nature, and especially of years, but we know nothing, since we came to this place, of lingering disease; this I esteem a comfort which demands corresponding gratitude to our Almighty preserver and benefactor.

"We have, in the second place, been delivered from the hand of the savage foe, who have been permitted to deal death and destruction to many families not far distant. 3d. We have been protected from the devouring element, which has often consumed in a few moments all that man could call his own on this whirling globe. 4th. Though not in affluence, we have a competency of such things as are needful. 5th. *We now have the Gospel preached every Sabbath*, and, although we have no evidences of awakenings among us, yet a degree of decorum and good order has prevailed which would do credit to some villages in the land of steady habits.

"Our social intercourse with our neighbors is mostly of a friendly character, and perhaps there is no place of the same size in our land where there is less poverty or absolute want than in Jacksonville; and if we do not recognize the good hand of God in all these mercies, it will be more tolerable for the land of Sodom and Gomorrah in the day of judgment than for us. A great moral improvement has taken place within the last two years. Profaneness, Sabbath-breaking, and intemperance abounded to an alarming degree when we first came here, and, although we can hardly say the people of Jacksonville are a church-going people, yet numbers do attend, let who will preach.

"It is a long time since I have heard of any new and extensive revivals of religion any where. Are Christians awake to this momentous concern? I sometimes fear, much fear, that the whole Church has become greatly conformed to the world, although it is so clearly enjoined upon us to set our affections on things above, and not on things of this world. St. James says, 'Whosoever will be a friend of the world is the enemy of God.' How should we take care in this, as well as all other matters that concern our usefulness here, and our everlasting destiny beyond the bounds of time and sense.

Let us pray for each other, and for all our dear friends, some of whom, we have reason to fear, are yet strangers to God and Christ, and in love with darkness. You, and I, and more of us have got far on our journey toward another world, and the admonition, 'Set thine house in order,' may, and ought to be listened to by us as a voice from God. I think I can say from the heart, with our favorite Watts, 'Heaven is before, and the world behind.'

" 'Lord, I renounce my carnal taste
Of the fair fruit that sinners prize;
Their paradise no more shall waste
One thought of mine, but to despise.

Come, heaven, and fill my vast desires;
My soul pursues the sovereign good:
She was all made of heavenly fires,
Nor can she live on meaner food.'

That the Lord, in mercy, may take charge of us all while we are sojourning here, and, through his abounding goodness in Christ Jesus, bring us, with all our dear friends, to meet in a better world, is the desire and prayer of your affectionate but unworthy brother,

"OBADIAH CONGAR."

In December of 1843, four others having united with Captain Congar in church-fellowship, they were duly organized into the First

Presbyterian Church of Jacksonville, in connection with the presbytery of Georgia, Rev. Mr. Baird, from St. Mary's, being present with them as a delegate from that body. Mr. William B. Barton and Captain Congar were at once elected and ordained elders. "The Sabbath day following," says the journal, "being the thirty-first of December, the significant and touching rite of the Lord's Supper was administered to our little number, and, at the same time, one new male member was added to the church by examination, viz., Stephen Eddy, from Massachusetts, for several years a resident of this village, making our whole number six. Thus ends the year 1843. The mercies and favors bestowed on me during the course of it have been like a running river: they have flowed on from the fountain of God's goodness without ever once stopping. Oh that my gratitude and obedience might correspond! How weighty, and yet, because of its sweetness, how light is the obligation which rests upon me, to consecrate the few remaining days I may yet have below to the service of my covenant-keeping God and Redeemer. Oh that I could realize my entire dependence on the grace of the Lord Jesus Christ to furnish me with every needed good for this world, but especially to furnish me with heavenly armor, that I may fight the battles of the Lord as a good soldier of Jesus Christ, and be enabled to resist every adversary that would oppose my march onward to a better world.

"Through Divine assistance, I am resolved, though old, to set out anew in this heavenly enterprise. But when I look back and see how many vows have been broken, how many resolutions to be more faithful, and more exemplary, and more consistent have fallen short, were it not for the promise of God to keep by his power, through faith unto salvation, all who have chosen him for their everlasting portion, my soul would sink into despondency. Through his grace, grace only, I hope to persevere unto the end. My soul, wait thou only, only, only upon God: my expectation is from him."

Oh, could I rule each erring thought,
  Each wrong desire subdue;
And serve my Maker as I ought,
  And thou wouldst have me do:
Oh, could I discipline my mind
  To seek the heavenly goal;
Nor strive in earthly things to find
  A treasure for the soul—
Then should my lips no more complain,
  Sin only makes my grief;
And Thou, that givest ease for pain,
  Wouldst quickly bring relief:

Ascendent over time and sense,
My feet should upward move,
Protected by thy providence,
Rejoicing in thy love.

"Monday, January 1st, 1844, finds me in the experience of countless blessings from my heavenly Father. My health, indeed, is not very good, but yet I enjoy much more than I suffer. My family has been spared to me, and I to them. Our worldly substance, though not increasing, is yet sufficient for our present wants; and we think, with good reason, the state of society is fast improving among us. There is now far less intemperance, Sabbath-breaking, and open vice and immorality here than when I came to this place. Preaching, also, is performed almost every Sabbath through the year. And now, if it be my Father's will to keep me here another year, may I be more humble, more meek, more patient, more engaged in the all-important duties of religion, in serving my God and Savior, and striving to do good to my fellow-men; bearing up under the trials of life without murmuring; submitting myself to my heavenly Father in all things; always keeping in mind that my final dissolution is drawing nigh, and that the great day of account is at hand."

Oh, may this thought possess my breast,
Where'er I rove, where'er I rest;
Nor let my weaker passions dare
Consent to sin, for God is there.

In April of this year Captain Congar was elected by his fellow-citizens to the office of Intendant, or Mayor, of Jacksonville. With his characteristic diffidence and self-distrust, he at first refused the honor; but his objections were overruled, and he filled the post, it is believed, with acceptance and good ability. His unaffected humility appears in the notice taken of it in his journal. It will have been observed, also, how uniformly the subject of this autobiography devoted the anniversaries of his birth to special reflection and review of his life and character as a man and a Christian. This habit he continued to the close of life; and when, in his last years, the entries are rare, birth-days are never omitted. At the close of his seventy-seventh year, we find him making this record in the words of the patriarch: "Few and evil have been the days of the years of my pilgrimage. Evil, not so much because my sufferings and afflictions have been great, but because of sin, the greatest evil. This has been the procuring cause of all other evils borne by me and by the rest of the human family. Yet to realize this mortifying truth is difficult. I find daily the infirmities of age gaining upon me. May I be suitably affected thereby, and henceforth keep my end in view more than ever I have yet done, and especially the *great end* of my existence in this world, the glory of God.

"It is not uncommon for a man to keep a record of the most important affairs and concerns of human life, and yet it is not common with men in general to record or notice particularly the day which ushered them into life and immortal being. I have often noticed, and sometimes with a deep interest, this era of my soul's beginning—at least interesting to my God and to me. My whole life, though of little account to the world at large, is of great and momentous account to myself. The very thought that I have an existence as a free moral agent, and that that existence will continue to all eternity, is a deeply interesting and momentous consideration to every one of the human family. What have I then to do in order that this existence may prove a blessing to myself as well as to my family and to all with whom I have to do? A man's way is said by Cecil to be declarative of his end. The wise man concludes his admonitions and exhortations thus: 'Let us hear the conclusion of the whole matter: fear

God and keep his commandments, for this is the whole duty of man.'

"Saturday, June 28th, 1845. Yesterday, the twenty-seventh, I commenced the seventy-eighth year of my age. My thoughts were occupied considerably on the goodness of God in sparing so great a sinner so many years, while thousands, to appearance far better than I, have long since been numbered with the dead. I stand a monument of the forbearance and patience of a holy God, and I have only to wonder that that patience has been so eminently extended to me, the chief of sinners, whom judgments and mercies did so long fail to soften. Glory to his sovereign grace that I was ever brought to submit."

Once I had a heart within,
  Thankless and opposed to God,
And, wandering in the ways of sin,
  In wisdom's ways had never trod.
Mercies were regarded not,
  Judgments came my soul to try,
But in a moment were forgot,
  And left me still to vanity.

But the spirit showed at last
  All the strictness of the Law,
And as its mirror o'er me pass'd,
  My heart's depravity I saw.
Then my soul, in deep despair,
  Felt within the rankling dart;

But Jesus pluck'd it out with care,
  And gave a renovated heart.
What I loved and sought before,
  Pleases me no longer now;
But at the cross my prayers I pour,
  At my Savior's feet I bow.

In the year 1846, the small band of Presbyterians at Jacksonville, being without a minister, were under the necessity of a conditional sale of their place of worship to the Methodists. Captain Congar had paid nearly three hundred dollars toward its erection, and it was a grief of mind to have to sell it, although to another evangelical society, who proffered them the use of it for public services at all times when a Presbyterian minister should be present. With a practical energy and zeal seldom evinced by one of his years, he now set about obtaining materials for building a small session and conference house on a lot of ground belonging to himself, for the purpose of holding prayer-meetings or other religious services when they should have a minister. To this end he solicited aid from friends in the North, and the following letters were written in that quest and in acknowledgment of donations.

"Jacksonville (E. F.), January 12th, 1847.

"My dear and beloved Sister,—I wrote

you on the first of December principally on a matter in which I have felt a deep interest. From the time I became acquainted with this place and with this people, it has been my constant study how, in what way, and when might means be obtained for the purpose of putting up a suitable building for the use of the Church —I mean, where Christians of all evangelical denominations could meet together to make their common supplications to the God of all mercy and grace, that he would be pleased to stop the flood-gates of vice and iniquity among us, pour out his Spirit, and revive his work in our parts.

In the solemn and regular attendance of the followers of our Lord and Savior Jesus Christ, a spirit of union and good feeling has often been witnessed, and we trust the prayers and praises of the people of God have been heard and answered. When I came to this place, it might well be called a sink of vice and open wickedness. Through the mercy and gracious interposition of the Great Head of the Church, vice and immorality have now received a check which I trust will continue; and could we get through and finish the building we have now under way, I hope a lasting blessing will yet arise to this community, which will continue when you and I have done with this world.

"Dear sister, I feel and am persuaded that it becomes us to work while the day lasts, for the night cometh when no man can work. I find myself failing in bodily strength, consequently I can do but little for the Church or for the world. My day is over for much effort in any case, yet I aim to do something for generations to come. I have a little property, a part of which I have consecrated for the service of God my Creator, preserver, and glorious Redeemer. It is indeed but little that I can do, but if this little be accepted, owned, and blessed, my desires will be granted. The building I am now erecting will seat between sixty and seventy persons, and is in a convenient part of the town; and we have reason to expect that when it is opened for worship, in a short time every seat will be occupied. My object, therefore, in writing you at this time is to solicit aid to help me through with this business. I can not obtain the aid which is needed in this place; and though you have manifested your good-will already, I hope you will respond to my request. It is not likely that either of us will need this world's goods much longer; and did I feel at perfect liberty to sell a portion of my property, I should at once do it, and devote the same to the purposes of religion and education here.

But your generosity and that of other friends, on whom I throw myself, may render it unnecessary. Confidently commending my request to you, and you to Him who loveth and who will bless the cheerful giver, I remain your sincere and affectionate brother,

"OBADIAH CONGAR."

"Jacksonville, February 9th, 1847.

"MY DEAR SISTER,—The receipt of a letter from our mutual friend, Mr. Woodruff, informing me that you had handed him thirty dollars as a contribution toward putting up a small place of worship which I am going on with, together with the advice that our female relative and friend Mrs. G. had also handed him five dollars for the same purpose, could not fail to produce emotions of gratitude to God our heavenly Father for his kind interposition in putting such thoughts of pious benevolence into the hearts of my dear friends at such a distance from me. And you, my dear sister, have peculiar claims of gratitude on my part, not simply for this act of liberality, but for the uniform and constant regard which you have manifested toward me ever since our first acquaintance.

"It is with much pleasure I reflect on the

relation which we hold to each other, and especially that relation which I trust will remain when time shall be no more. Give my sincere thanks to Mrs. G. for her precious gift, which will do much toward aiding me in completing the work I have undertaken. For your information, as well as for others who may take an interest in the cause of religion in Jacksonville, I would state, that the building is now under cover and the glass in, and I have the satisfaction to say that my neighbors, and others friendly to religious institutions, think the house well adapted to the purposes for which it has been erected, namely, for holding social prayer-meetings in.

"For want of a suitable place to hold such meetings, the numbers who have attended for the last two years past have been very small. One of the evil consequences of holding prayer-meetings in a private house is, that the individuals who come together on these occasions are mostly of the same class. In the public place of worship none will be shut out. But now, dear sister, don't feel as though you had nothing more to do, but, I beseech you, plead most fervently that the blessing of the God of Israel may descend upon this weak and feeble institution, that the hearts of all who may attend may be united together in love, and that the spirit of grace may enlighten the minds of the unregenerate, and stir up Christians of all denominations to more active zeal and engagedness in the cause of their Lord and Master; and oh, remember your unworthy brother and his companion, that she too may become a humble follower of the Lord Jesus. You are aware that we have lived together over fifty-one years, and yet I fear she is a stranger to true religion. In the course of nature, it can not be that we shall much longer abide together in this earthly tent. May we only be fitted to live and reign together with Christ in glory. Separation for eternity would be sad indeed, and yet is there not reason to fear that will be, unless we both have the uniting bond to Christ? For myself, it is a pleasant thought that my time here can be but short. Life I am not weary of, but I often long to be with Jesus.

"I BID my hours to hasten on,
That I may be where Christ has gone;
With him I long in heaven to meet,
To pay my honors at his feet.
Oh thou bless'd Savior! thou dost see
How sad my heart, when far from thee!
Though here on earth thy love I share,
Yet I had rather see thee there.

Thou said'st, before thy feet were set
Upon their march from Olivet,
What time the clouds and heavens of light
Received thee from the gazer's sight,
That thou didst go, that there might be
A place prepared for us and Thee.
Oh, fit me for that dwelling-place,
Where I shall see thee face to face."

Chapter XIII.

CLOSING YEARS, DEATH, AND RETROSPECT OF CHARACTER.

Joy, joy to the soul that is ripe for ascending
  If hope be the star that enlightens death's vale;
For why should we keep it from joys never ending,
  To tenant this mansion of weeping and wail?
Its stains, wash'd away by the full crimson gushes
  From the wounded Redeemer, no longer remain;
On the wings of an angel to heaven it rushes,
  To be happy forever, and ever to reign.

The Departing Christian.

Port is almost gained; the voyage of life is well-nigh up; the Christian mariner's Snug Harbor is nearly entered; eternal glory opens to the view;

Christian, cast anchor now,
  Heaven is thy home.

We have followed the thread of this autobiography till it is all but spent, carefully unraveling and winding it off at intervals, and weaving it up with an appropriate woof into the tissue of this book. But little remains to complete our fabric and lift it from the loom. The two last years of Captain Congar's life, although he continued in active business, were, on the whole, composed and peaceful above any that had gone before. At the close of his seventy-eighth year we find him making this cheerful entry in his journal:

"I record this day that the same Good Hand which has taken care of me through childhood, youth, and riper age, has carried me deep into the vale of years, even to the closing day of the seventy-eighth year of my life. And here I would express my gratitude to my Almighty Preserver and Benefactor that I have wanted for no good thing. My general health through the year has been better than for some years past, and no evil has befallen me or any of my family, except that my wife has lost the sight, in a great degree, of her right eye. We, however, have abundant reason to be thankful, none to complain. Why, but of his sovereign grace, has He so highly favored us!"

O, to grace how great a debtor,
  Daily I'm constrain'd to be!
Let that grace now, like a fetter,
  Bind my wand'ring soul to thee.

"How does it now become me more than ever to consecrate all my faculties and days that remain to my God and Redeemer. Oh, how poor a return for all his goodness! Had I a thousand lives to live, and a thousand hearts to give, they should be all devoted to him. But 'tis only this one poor offering I can now make."

> Here, Lord, I give myself away!
> 'Tis all that I can do.

"June 27th, 1847. To-day begins the eightieth year of my earthly pilgrimage. How strange that I should have navigated so long without shipwreck that stormy sea of life on which millions of barks, freighted with immortality, that sailed with me, have long since foundered! When I ask, why is it so, my heart replies, not for any thing in me, but 'Even so, Father, for so it seemed good in thy sight.' My Savior has been at the helm."

> He is my Pilot wise;
> My compass is his word;
> My soul all storms defies,
> While I have such a Lord!
> I trust his faithfulness and power,
> To save me in the trying hour.

"Hitherto the Lord hath helped me; my shortcomings and his long-suffering have gone together until now; but methinks my heart hopes and resolves to be his entirely henceforth and forever. God has not only kept the taper of my life burning so long, but he has spared my family to me another year, and the health of us all has been far better than we could have expected. My life in the retrospect looks black as ever, but so does the grace of Christ look brighter than ever, and therefore I do not despair and moan as I once did. For one thought to myself, I now, like holy Baxter, give many thoughts to my adorable Savior, for in him is all my comfort and peace. '*God is in Christ reconciling the world to himself, not imputing their trespasses to them;*' and here is encouragement enough, together with that blessed word, '*Him that cometh unto me I will in no wise cast out,*' for trembling sinners like me every where to lay hold of. But ah! the unbelief that hangs so heavy, and makes us slow of heart to embrace the encouragements held out to us in the promises. How many pious souls go mourning without cause all their days, as I have done till near fourscore; not so much mourning for their sins, as that they find so little comfort in religion, when they are all the time looking into themselves for grounds of comfort in their exercises and acts, instead of looking aloft to the Lord Jesus Christ, the only possible ground of true comfort to a sin-sorrowing soul. Oh! had I learned this secret earlier of looking always to Jesus, how much more I should have enjoyed; how much happier I might have been as a Christian all my days. I have found it to be only union with Christ by faith, and a constant recollection of him as a present Savior, that can keep the soul happy by keeping it from sin."

Oh, sacred union with the Perfect Mind!
  Transcendent bliss, which thou alone canst give!
How bless'd are they this pearl of price who find,
  And, dead to earth, have learned in thee to live.

Thus, in thine arms of love, oh God, I lie,
  Now and forever lost to all but thee;
My happy soul, since it hath learn'd to die,
  Hath found new life in thine infinity.

Oh, go and learn this lesson of the Cross,
  And tread the way which saints and prophets trod,
Who, counting life, and self, and all things loss,
  Have found in inward death the life of God.

"October 14, 1847. The return of this day reminds me of my narrow escape from drowning fifty years ago, through the mercy of God, while the ship I was attached to lay at Canton. How vivid is the remembrance of it, although my heart is not so deeply affected at this distance by calling to mind the goodness of my Almighty Deliverer in this instance as it ought to be. Ease did soon recant vows made in pain, but it was not forgotten, nor its effect wholly lost as a part of my heavenly Father's discipline to bring me to himself. 'He it was that took me and drew me out of many waters, and saved me for his mercy's sake.' "

'Tis to his power I owe my breath,
And all my near escapes from death.

The following extracts from a letter dated at Jacksonville, November 25th, 1847, furnish the only remaining personal and domestic items to be recorded of Captain Congar's residence and employments in Florida:

" Dear and beloved Sister,—My heart has been inditing you a letter for some weeks past, and I must begin with what my heart is full of, the goodness of God. My Mary and I, Darby and Joan like, are sitting together in our little dining-room. And, first, I desire to be thankful to Almighty God, our heavenly Father, for his protecting care over us, and the numerous and unmerited favors which we have, through all our journeyings by sea and by land, received at his gracious hand. And it especially becomes us on this day, which has been recommended by the governor of this state to be observed by all its citizens as a day of public thanksgiving for all the mercies which a gracious Providence has bestowed on us as a young member of the great confederacy, and for the blessings heaped upon our whole land as a people—I say, then, on this occasion, *we* are called upon to record on our hearts the goodness of God in bringing us thus far on the journey of life, even to advanced age, and still rendering our circumstances in life far more comfortable than with millions as good or better than we. We have a convenient dwelling, situated about one hundred and eighty yards from the River St. John's, with the beef and fish market in full view from our house, and the same distance from it. The market-bell is always rung to notify when either of the above articles are for sale. Our market has generally been well supplied with both these necessaries at very cheap prices. We get the best cut of the hind quarter, whether for steaks or roasting, at six and a quarter cents per pound, and we can rarely consume six and a quarter cents' worth of excellent fish for dinner. We purchase the best kind of wood at two dollars and fifty cents per cord, delivered at our yard. Vegetables, the growth of the country, are scarce, except sweet potatoes, now thirty-seven and a half cents per bushel. Our family numbers only three, viz., Mary, myself, and our domestic, named Lydia, now about fifty years of age.

"Our expenses would be within our income, were it not for the large outlay of our yearly travel North. We have a competence, and with that are content. He, I know, who feeds the young ravens when they cry, will supply me and mine with all things needful as long as we shall want. But, if it would not be inconsistent to desire more, I would that I had it, in order to *do more* for the support of the Gospel, and the religious institutions in this section of our country. As a little family, we get along very quietly together. We seldom exchange visits except with a few particular friends. Our habits have become quite domestic. This is true of us all; even our servant seems to have taken a pattern by us in these respects. We perceive a great alteration in her habits for the better.

"I will now turn my thoughts a little on the state of religion in this community, and its attending privileges. I believe that I have already apprised you that the Presbyterian clergyman who had been sent here by the Presbytery of Georgia left us twelve months ago last April, since which we have had no minister of our own denomination with us except a few Sabbaths. The Presbytery of Georgia signified to us more than a year since that they could not find a man to send us, adding, at the same time, that there are now more than six hundred organized churches under the care of the Board of Missions for which they were not able to furnish pastors. When I received this information, I was compelled to draw the conclusion that our case was hopeless. The discouraging statements of the Presbytery and of the Board of Missions in Philadelphia led us to the determination to sell the Church property to the Methodist Society. This measure I now fully approve, and am satisfied that the result has been favorable both toward uniting Christians of different denominations in their feelings, and in their efforts to promote religion among us.

The state of things in these respects is far better than it has been at any time since I became a resident here. These are the outward advantages, then, which the whole community have obtained by the purchase of the Baptist church by myself and two other Presbyterians, which we did to save it from falling into the hands of worldly men to speculate upon, or use for secular purposes. And then, again, for want of sufficient aid to support a minister and to keep the building from decay, we were obliged to transfer the property to the Methodist people. All this has been (I consider) providential, and was well done on our part, for we have secured for this people a convenient house of worship, which might not have been the case otherwise. It is true I was necessarily obliged to advance myself more than two hundred dollars toward the purchase of the building, but this amount, together with what I collected when in New York, and the donations so liberally and timely forwarded us by yourself and cousin, have put it in my power to erect a convenient and suitable building for the purpose of holding a weekly prayer-meeting in, where we unite with our brethren of other denominations for worship. I contemplate making a deed of this property to the Churches. I am further happy to say that the Methodist minister who labors among us has done much to raise the standard of religion and Christian fellowship, and has been the means of calling out many to attend religious services who heretofore have stood aloof from the house of worship. The seats being free, the rich and poor meet together. With respect to my own religious feelings, exercises, hopes, and expectations, I would only remark that, on the whole, I trust I possess a more abiding sense of my unworthiness and insufficiency, and that I wait with a comfortable assurance of eternal life, only through the unmerited mercy of God in Christ Jesus, the great Redeemer.

"A few thoughts concerning the present calamity with which as a nation we are sorely chastised—I mean, the war now going on between our government and the republic of Mexico. I profess not to be a prophet; yet I did firmly believe that, should Texas be annexed to the United States, it would certainly result in a war with Mexico. I mentioned this my full persuasion to numbers around me; and, besides, I could not fall in with the policy of our government in seeking to extend our territory so far, believing that, even if this new state should be added by mutual agreement, as well of Mexico as of Texas, that even then we should only involve ourselves with new cares and difficulties, which could never be balanced by any advantages to be gained. But when we reflect upon the horrors occasioned by this impolitic step; when we reflect upon the increase of vice and immorality which prevails when men are congregated together by thousands, destitute of the restraints of religion, and far from the society of the good and virtuous, what can we expect. But the melancholy loss of life and the sorrows of the sick and wounded make up a dreadful tale of woe. We know, to be sure, that God can overrule all these awful events for the advancement of his kingdom in this world; but man meaneth not so. It is my consolation that God reigns, and that his kingdom is yet visibly coming on earth. We and our nation are in the hands of the All-mighty and All-wise. He will do with us and for us that which is best and for his own glory. To Him be endless praises. Amen."

During the year 1848, the last of Captain Congar's mortal life, there are but two scraps of autobiographical annals which reflect any light upon his experience and habits as a man of God. The first is at the opening of the year; the second, as usual, on the anniversary of his birth.

"January 2d, 1848. Not one day have I seen from my earliest recollection but what I have been called upon to acknowledge the good hand of my God. But especially at the commencement of a new year is it both a duty and a joy to raise a pillar of gratitude to the Lord's goodness. On this occasion I would notice with thankfulness the kindness of my heavenly Father in bringing me low and then raising me up. The Psalmist says, 'I was brought low, and He helped me;' and my experience has been his over again. In the month of July I had a severe return of dyspepsy; but my affliction was short; I was soon restored, and have been favored with better health than I had known for some time; and I have found by experience that strict temperance in eating, as well as drinking, is essential to good health. I am therefore resolved more than ever to attend to this lesson, since the doing of all in my power for the maintenance of body and mind in vigor while I remain below is a duty I owe both to God and to my fellow-men."

Master, I own thy lawful claim,
  Thine, wholly thine, I long to be!
Thou seest at last I willing am,
  Where'er thou goest, to follow thee:
Myself in all things to deny;
Thine, only thine, to live and die.

Whate'er my sinful flesh requires,
  For thee I cheerfully forego;
My covetous and vain desires,
  My hopes of happiness below;
My senses' and my passions' food,
And all my thirst for creature good.

Pleasure, and wealth, and praise no more
  Shall lead my captive soul astray;
My fond pursuits I all give o'er,
  Thee, only thee, resolv'd t' obey:
My own in all things to resign,
And know no other will but thine.

"It is easy, comparatively, for an old man like me to adopt this. Oh, that I had been all this from my earliest days! What but grace did keep me from ruin by my sins in early life! I am a wonder to myself, my lamp of life holding out so long. I stand a monument of the Divine mercy; and I would have my epitaph,

A SINNER SAVED BY GRACE.

"June 29th, 1848. Day before yesterday was the birth-day of my eighty-first year. I try in vain to realize that I have lived so long, that I have been so many years a fixture in this changing world, outliving almost all that began with me the race of life. I often wonder why it is that the most unworthy of my father's house should be spared the longest. All my brothers, one of them younger than I, have years ago gone down to the tomb, while I still enjoy a good degree of health, though subject to the infirmities of age, and at times feeling great weakness of body, especially in my knees. But I have every thing to be grateful for, both as regards my spiritual and my temporal condition. In general, I have been favored of late years with a comfortable hope, which I trust is spiritual, that, whenever it shall please God to call me away from this sublunary scene, I shall be permitted to meet again with many dear friends who have gone to heaven before me, and, above all, to see His face who died for the sins of many, and now reigns in glory. Till I get to the mansion which He has prepared for all those who love Him, may I, by walking daily with God as Enoch did, recommend my religion to all with whom I have to do, and be enabled to bear up under all the troubles of this mortal life with a holy confidence in the truth and faithfulness of my covenant God and Father, through the intercession of the Lord Jesus Christ. Amen and Amen."

Heav'n is my house and portion fair;
My treasure and my heart are there,
And my abiding home:
For me my elder brethren stay,
And angels beckon me away,
And Jesus bids me come.

I go, thy servant, Lord, replies;
I go to meet thee in the skies,
And claim my heavenly rest:
Now let the pilgrim's journey end;
Now, O my Savior, Brother, Friend,
Receive me to thy breast!

The personal memorials of our pilgrim-mariner are now ended, and it remains only briefly to record the manner of his death, and to present a short synopsis of his character and virtues as viewed by his friends and gathered from the foregoing annals. The same summer with the last date above, he visited the North, as it was his custom to do; and, although his aspect of health and activity was the general remark of his friends, the impression was fixed upon his own mind that this visit was to be his last. While in the city of New York, he was seized suddenly with erysipelas, on Thursday, September 14th, and died the next week on Friday.

Almost simultaneously with the setting in of the disease, his brain was so affected that he was thought to be sensible at only two short intervals of time. His constitution was one in which the sympathy was more immediate and apparent than in the majority of cases between the body and mind, and thence probably the liability which we have observed to great depression when his health was at all impaired during his lifetime. In his sickness he appeared not to suffer pain, the dread of which was one of his peculiarities in health. His final exit was easy, and he passed into peace. In the lines of his favorite, Charles Wesley,

The voyage of life 's at an end,
The mortal affliction is past,
The age that in heaven he'll spend
Forever and ever shall last.

His funeral took place in Newark, New Jersey, and his remains were conveyed to the first Presbyterian church burying-ground by a large concourse of attached friends and relatives, there to wait THE RESURRECTION OF THE JUST.

Rest, Christian, rest! thy warfare is done,
Thou hast fought the good fight, and the victory won.

In making out a brief synopsis of the character developed in the foregoing autobiography and memorials, and as it appeared to the eyes of friends, we are reminded of the remark of Wordsworth, that the character of a deceased friend or beloved kinsman ought not to be seen otherwise than as a tree through a tender haze or luminous mist, that spiritualizes and beautifies it; that takes away, indeed, but only to the end that the parts not abstracted may appear more dignified and lovely, may impress and affect the more.

Let us, then, concisely sketch that character as it is given by friends that knew its virtues, and were not blind to its faults. 1. His manners. He was polite in his intercourse with all: his words and ways were marked by a gentlemanly civility and kindness. He was obliging, affectionate, social, and sympathizing outwardly, because within there was the frank, noble heart of a true Christian sailor, which was ever ready to recognize a brother in a fellow-man. In his dress, also, and personal appearance he was scrupulously neat and decorous, even to ripe fourscore.

2. Integrity of character and benevolence. Those who knew him little, trusted him, and those who knew him best were never disappointed or deceived in this sterling virtue. He had that conscientious regard for his word and for the interests of others that always belongs to an upright mind, and that carries conviction of it to others. As commander of a ship, and intrusted by his employers with lives and property, he secured their highest confidence, and was no less beloved and trusted by his men. Always unassuming and unaspiring, others thought far more of his faithfulness than he did of himself.

As a merchant, his *honesty* far surpassed the standard of the present day. Exact in business—fulfilling all engagements and promises—his word was uniformly regarded as truth. It was a rule with him never to purchase an article of merchandise that he knew was not good, and never to sell an article for what he knew it was not; and hence it followed that the poor man, the slave, and all who traded with him, held him in so high esteem and affection. The grand principle that regulated his conduct was of divine origin: "All things whatsoever ye would that men should do to you, do ye even so to them." A reasonable profit was all that *he would have*, although often he might have had more, and under circumstances in which the most of men would have taken more. He has therefore left behind him a savor of honesty, integrity, and singleness of purpose wherever he went, that is his best eulogium.

This implies, also, benevolence, which shone in him brightly as a trait of character, both in large matters and in small, making him kind to the poor and friendless, and generous, up to his ability, to every good cause. Although heavily drawn upon at home, he was always giving to the great benevolent objects of the day. The ground for a session-house at Jacksonville he gave outright, and erected the building upon it. One of his last acts before he left the place was to give a deed to the Presbyterian Church, conveying all his interest in the building and land. Impressed with the uncertainty of life, when about to leave for his last visit to the North, and when urged by friends not to trouble himself about it, he refused to leave till he had effected the conveyance. He was a liberal contributor to the Seamen's Friend Society and to the American Board, and the final disposal of his property by will is to those societies.

3. His Christian principle and piety. On ship and shore, wherever he went, on deck or port, he made himself known as a Christian, and it was seen that he loved and was not ashamed of THE FRIEND OF SINNERS. We have learned by the foregoing memorials how he made it a matter of conscience neither to leave port nor to make sail on the Sabbath. He was deemed a favorite of Providence, and his scruples never cost him a berth, or even at all endangered his discharge, for it used to be said among owners that a special superintending Providence always took care of him and his ship.

It has been seen that his piety was an active and working piety, and how carefully he looked after the religious interests of his men at sea, and of his neighbors on the land. As to his own personal enjoyment of religion, for a large part of his life he was what is called a doubting Christian, owing chiefly to constitutional peculiarities. Like truly modest persons always, he thought less favorably of his own piety than others did. But it will have been observed with pleasure by the sympathizing reader how it assumed a more cheerful aspect, and a tone of greater assurance, as his pilgrimage drew to a close.

4. His end. His sun grew larger at its

setting, and his evidences and hope of heaven became brighter as his shadow fell longer on the plain of life. Friends noted the change, and admired in him the grace of the Redeemer ripening him for glory. When at length he was gathered, it was as a shock of corn fully ripe in its season. Grace had gone so far in its work of renovation as to correct natural corruptions, acidity, and bitterness,

> "And lay the paths of peevish nature even;"

and, though neither eminently great, or wise or lovely, he was, notwithstanding, greatly beloved by the friends who knew him, and they are confident he has entered into the joy of the Lord. "A man's way is declarative of his end." "MARK THE PERFECT, AND BEHOLD THE UPRIGHT, FOR THE END OF THAT MAN IS PEACE."

May the earnest minds of both landsmen and mariners, who shall have been induced to follow us through these simple memorials, be emulous of the virtues and wary of the faults herein portrayed; and when *our* voyage of life is over, and friends lay us in the narrow house appointed for all the living, may it be said of each friendly *reader* of these annals, with as much confidence as it could be spoken of their subject,

He has gone into peace; he has laid him down
  To sleep till the dawn of a brighter day:
And he shall awake on that holy morn,
  When sorrow and sighing shall flee away.

THE END.

Louisiana
Its Colonial History and Romance. By CHARLES GAYARRE, Esq. 8vo, Muslin.

Lord Holland's Foreign Reminiscences.
Edited by his Son, HENRY EDWARD LORD HOLLAND. 12mo, Muslin.

The Pictorial Field-Book of the Revolu-
tion; or, Illustrations by Pen and Pencil, of the History, Scenery, Biography, Relics, and Traditions of the War for Independence. By BENSON J. LOSSING, Esq. Embellished with 500 Engravings on Wood, chiefly from Original Sketches by the Author. In about 20 Numbers, 8vo, Paper, 25 cents each.

Life and Writings of Thomas Chalmers,
D.D., LL.D. Edited by his Son-in-Law, Rev. WILLIAM HANNA, LL.D. 3 vols. 12mo, Paper, 75 cents; Muslin, $1 00 per Volume.

Life of John Calvin.
Compiled from authentic Sources, and particularly from his Correspondence. By THOMAS H. DYER. Portrait. 12mo, Muslin, $1 00.

Leigh Hunt's Autobiography,
With Reminiscences of Friends and Contemporaries 2 vols. 12mo, Muslin, $1 50.

Southey's Life and Correspondence.
Edited by his Son, Rev. CHARLES CUTHBERT SOUTHEY, M.A. In 6 Parts, 8vo, Paper, 25 cents each; one Volume, Muslin, $2 00.

Dr. Johnson: his Religious Life and his
Death. 12mo, Muslin, $1 00.

Life and Letters of Thomas Campbell.
Edited by WILLIAM BEATTIE, M.D., one of his Executors. With an Introductory Letter by WASHINGTON IRVING, Esq. Portrait. 2 vols. 12mo, Muslin, $2 50.

Benjamin Franklin's Autobiography.
With a Sketch of his Public Services, by Rev. H. HASTINGS WELD. With numerous exquisite Designs, by JOHN G. CHAPMAN. 8vo, Muslin, $2 50; Sheep, $2 75; half Calf, $3 00.

Hume's History of England,

From the Invasion of Julius Cæsar to the Abdication of James II., 1688. A new Edition, with the Author's last Corrections and Improvements. To which is prefixed a short Account of his Life, written by Himself. With a Portrait of the Author. 6 vols. 12mo, Cloth, $2 40; Sheep, $3 00.

Macaulay's History of England,

From the Accession of James II. With an original Portrait of the Author. Vols. I. and II. Library Edition, 8vo, Muslin, 75 cents per Volume; Sheep extra, 87½ cents per Volume; Calf backs and corners, $1 00 per Volume.—Cheap Edition, 8vo, Paper, 25 cents per Volume.—12mo (uniform with Hume), Cloth, 40 cents per Volume.

Gibbon's History of Rome,

With Notes, by Rev. H. H. Milman and M. Guizot. Maps and Engravings. 4 vols. 8vo, Sheep extra, $5 00. —A new Cheap Edition, with Notes by Rev. H. H. Milman. To which is added a complete index of the whole Work and a Portrait of the Author. 6 vols. 12mo (uniform with Hume), Cloth, $2 40; Sheep, $3 00.

Journal and Memorials of Capt. Obadiah

Congar: for Fifty Years Mariner and Shipmaster from the Port of New York. By Rev. H. T. Cheever. 16mo, Muslin.

History of Spanish Literature.

With Criticisms on the particular Works and Biographical Notices of prominent Writers. By George Ticknor, Esq. 3 vols. 8vo, half Calf extra, $7 50; Sheep extra, $6 75; Muslin, $6 00.

History of the National Constituent As-

sembly, from May, 1848. By J. F. Corkran, Esq. 12mo, Muslin, 90 cents; Paper, 75 cents.

The Recent Progress of Astronomy,

especially in the United States. By Elias Loomis, M.A. 12mo, Muslin, $1 00.

The English Language

In its Elements and Forms. With a History of its Origin and Development, and a full Grammar. By W. C. Fowler, M.A. 8vo, Muslin, $1 50; Sheep, $1 75.

History of Ferdinand and Isabella.

By William H. Prescott, Esq. 3 vols. 8vo, half Calf, $7 50; Sheep extra, $6 75; Muslin, $6 00.

History of the Conquest of Mexico.

With the Life of the Conqueror, Hernando Cortez, and a View of the Ancient Mexican Civilization. By William H. Prescott, Esq. Portrait and Maps. 3 vols. 8vo, half Calf, $7 50; Sheep extra, $6 75; Muslin, $6 00.

History of the Conquest of Peru.

With a Preliminary view of the Civilization of the Incas. By William H. Prescott, Esq. Portraits, Maps, &c. 2 vols. 8vo, half Calf, $5 00; Sheep extra, $4 50; Muslin, $4 00.

Biographical and Critical Miscellanies.

Containing Notices of Charles Brockden Brown, the American Novelist.—Asylum for the Blind.—Irving's Conquest of Grenada. Cervantes.—Sir W. Scott.—Chauteaubriand's English Literature. — Bancroft's United States.—Madame Calderon's Life in Mexico.—Moliere.—Italian Narrative Poetry.—Poetry and Romance of the Italians.—Scottish Song.—Da Ponte's Observations. By William H. Prescott, Esq. Portrait. 8vo, Muslin, $2 00; Sheep extra, $2 25; half Calf, $2 50.

The Conquest of Canada.

By the Author of "Hochelaga." 2 vols. 12mo, Muslin, $1 70.

Past, Present, and Future of the Republic.

By Alphonse de Lamartine. 12mo, Muslin, 50 cents; Paper, 37½ cents.

The War with Mexico.

By R. S. Ripley, U.S.A. With Maps, Plans of Battles, &c. 2 vols. 12mo, Muslin, $4 00; Sheep, $4 50; half Calf, $5 00.

History of the Confessional.

By John Henry Hopkins, D.D., Bishop of Vermont 12mo, Muslin, $1 00.

Dark Scenes of History.

By G. P. R. James, Esq. 12mo, Muslin, $1 00; Paper, 75 cents

Life and Writings of Washington;

Being his Correspondence, Addresses, Messages, and other Papers, Official and Private, selected and published from the original Manuscripts, with a Life of the Author, and Notes and Illustrations, &c. By JARED SPARKS, LL.D. With numerous Engravings. 12 vols. 8vo, Muslin, $18 00; Sheep extra, $21 00; half Calf, $24 00.

Library of American Biography.

Edited by JARED SPARKS, LL.D. Portraits, &c. 10 vols. 12mo, Muslin, $7 50. Each volume sold separately, if desired, price 75 cents.

Gieseler's Ecclesiastical History.

From the Fourth Edition, revised and amended. Translated from the German, by SAMUEL DAVIDSON, LL.D. Vols. I. and II., 8vo, Muslin, $3 00.

History of the American Bible Society.

From its Organization in 1816 to the Present Time. By Rev. W. P. STRICKLAND. With an Introduction, by Rev. N. L. RICE, and a Portrait of Hon. ELIAS BOUDINOT, LL.D., first President of the Society. 8vo, Sheep, $1 75; Cloth, $1 50.

Biographical History of Congress:

Comprising Memoirs of Members of the Congress of the United States, together with a History of Internal Improvements from the Foundation of the Government to the Present Time. By HENRY G. WHEELER. With Portraits and Fac-simile Autographs. 8vo, Muslin, $3 00 per Volume.

Schmitz's History of Rome,

From the Earliest Times to the Death of Commodus, A.D. 192. With Questions, by JOHN ROBSON, B.A. 18mo, Muslin, 75 cents.

Louis the Fourteenth,

and the Court of France in the Seventeenth Century. By MISS PARDOE. Illustrated with numerous Engravings, Portraits, &c. 2 vols. 12mo, Muslin, $3 50.

History of the Girondists;

Or, Personal Memoirs of the Patriots of the French Revolution. By A. DE LAMARTINE. From unpublished Sources. 3 vols. 12mo, Muslin, $2 10.

Josephus's Complete Works.

A new Translation, by Rev. Robert Traill, D.D. With Notes, Explanatory Essays, &c., by Rev. Isaac Taylor, of Ongar. Illustrated by numerous Engravings. Publishing in Monthly Numbers, 8vo, Paper, 25 cents each.

History of the French Revolution.

By Thomas Carlyle. Newly Revised by the Author, with Index, &c. 2 vols. 12mo, Muslin, $2 00.

Letters and Speeches of Cromwell.

With Elucidations and connecting Narrative. By T. Carlyle. 2 vols. 12mo, Muslin, $2 00.

Life of Madame Guyon.

Life and Religious Opinions of Madame Guyon: together with some Account of the Personal History and Religious Opinions of Archbishop Fenelon. By T. C. Upham. 2 vols. 12mo, Muslin, $2 00.

Life of Madame Catharine Adorna.

Including some leading Facts and Traits in her Religious Experience. Together with Explanations and Remarks, tending to illustrate the Doctrine of Holiness. 12mo, Muslin, gilt edges, 60 cents; Muslin, 50 cents.

Homes and Haunts of the British Poets.

By William Howitt. With numerous Illustrations. 2 vols. 12mo, Muslin, $3 00.

History of Wonderful Inventions.

Illustrated by numerous Engravings. 12mo, Muslin, 75 cents; Paper, 50 cents.

The Valley of the Mississippi.

History of the Discovery and Settlement of the Valley of the Mississippi, by the three great European Powers, Spain, France, and Great Britain; and the subsequent Occupation, Settlement, and Extension of Civil Government by the United States, until the year 1846. By John W. Monette, Esq. Maps. 2 vols. 8vo, Muslin, $5 00; Sheep, $5 50.

Life and Writings of Cassius M. Clay;

Including Speeches and Addresses. Edited, with a Preface and Memoir, by Horace Greeley. With Portrait. 8vo, Muslin, $1 50.

The Incarnation ;

Or, Pictures of the Virgin and her Son. By the Rev CHARLES BEECHER. With an introductory Essay, by Mrs. HARRIET B. STOWE. 18mo, Muslin,

Blackstone's Commentaries on the

Laws of England. With the last Corrections of the Author, and Notes from the Twenty-first London Edition. With copious Notes explaining the Changes in the Law effected by Decision or Statute down to 1844. Together with Notes adapting the Work to the American Student, by J. L. WENDELL, Esq. With a Memoir of the Author. 4 vols. 8vo, Sheep extra, $7 00.

Letters, Conversations, and Recollec

tions of S. T. Coleridge. 12mo, Muslin, 65 cents.

Specimens of the Table-talk of S. T

Coleridge. Edited by H. N. COLERIDGE. 12mo, Muslin, 70 cents.

Mardi : and a Voyage Thither.

By HERMAN MELVILLE. 2 vols. 12mo, Muslin, $1 75

Omoo ;

Or, a Narrative of Adventures in the South Seas By HERMAN MELVILLE. 12mo, Muslin, $1 25.

Burke's complete Works.

With a Memoir. Portrait. 3 vols. 8vo, Sheep extra, $5 00.

Montgomery's Lectures on General Lit-

erature, Poetry, &c., with a Retrospect of Literature, and a View of modern English Literature. 18mo, Muslin, 45 cents.

Boswell's Life of Dr. Johnson.

Including a Journal of a Tour to the Hebrides. With numerous Additions and Notes, by J. W. CROKER, LL.D. A new Edition, entirely revised, with much additional Matter. With a Portrait. 2 vols. 8vo, Muslin, $2 75 ; Sheep extra, $3 00.

Dr. Samuel Johnson's complete Works.

With an Essay on his Life and Genius, by A. MURPHY, Esq. A new, revised Edition. With Engravings. 2 vols. 8vo, Muslin, $2 75; Sheep extra, $3 00.

Cicero's Offices, Orations, &c.

The Orations translated by DUNCAN; the Offices, by COCKMAN; and the Cato and Lelius, by MELMOTH. With a Portrait. 3 vols. 18mo, Muslin, $1 25.

Paley's Natural Theology.

A new Edition, from large Type, edited by D. E. BARTLETT. Copiously Illustrated, and a Life and Portrait of the Author. 2 vols. 12mo, Muslin, $1 50.

Paley's Natural Theology.

With illustrative Notes, &c., by Lord BROUGHAM and Sir C. BELL, and preliminary Observations and Notes, by ALONZO POTTER, D.D. With Engravings. 2 vols. 18mo, Muslin, 90 cents

The Orations of Demosthenes.

Translated by THOMAS LELAND, D.D. 2 vols. 18mo, Muslin, 85 cents.

Potter's Hand-book for Readers and Students,

intended to assist private Individuals, Associations, School Districts, &c., in the Selection of useful and interesting Works for Reading and Investigation. 18mo, Muslin, 45 cents.

Dendy's Philosophy of Mystery.

12mo, Muslin, 50 cents.

Hoes and Way's Anecdotical Olio.

Anecdotes, Literary, Moral, Religious, and Miscellaneous. 8vo, Muslin, $1 00.

Lamb's Works.

Comprising his Letters, Poems, Essays of Elia, Essays upon Shakespeare, Hogarth, &c., and a Sketch of his Life, by T. NOON TALFOURD. With a Portrait 2 vols. royal 12mo, Muslin. $2 00.

Amenities of Literature;

Consisting of Sketches and Characters of English Literature. By I. D'Israeli, D.C.L., F.S.A. 2 vols. 12mo, Muslin, $1 50.

Dryden's complete Works.

With a Memoir. Portrait. 2 vols. 8vo, Sheep extra, $3 75.

Woman in America;

Being an Examination into the Moral and Intellectual Condition of American Female Society. By Mrs. A. J. Graves. 18mo, Muslin, 45 cents.

Homes and Haunts of the most eminent

British Poets. By William Howitt. With numerous Illustrations. 2 vols. 12mo, Muslin, $3 00.

Mrs. Jameson's Visits and Sketches at

Home and Abroad. Including the "Diary of an Ennuyée." 2 vols. 12mo, Muslin, $1 00.

The Sacred Philosophy of the Seasons.

Illustrating the Perfections of God in the Phenomena of the Year. By Rev. Henry Duncan, D.D. With important Additions, and some Modifications to adapt it to American Readers, by F. W. P. Greenwood, D.D. 4 vols. 12mo, Muslin, $3 00.

Mackenzie's Novels and Miscellaneous

Works, comprising The Man of Feeling, The Man of the World, Julia de Roubigne, &c. With a Memoir of the Author, by Sir Walter Scott. Royal 12mo, Muslin, $1 00.

How to Observe.

Morals and Manners. By Miss Harriet Martineau 12mo, Muslin, 42½ cents.

The Spoon.

With upward of 100 Illustrations, Primitive, Egyptian, Roman, Mediæval, and Modern. By H. O. Westman. 8vo, Muslin, $1 25.

A New Spirit of the Age.

Edited by R. H. Horne. 12mo, Paper, 25 cents.

Men, Women, and Books.

A Selection of Sketches, Essays, and Critical Memoirs, from his uncollected Prose Writings. By Leigh Hunt. 2 vols. 12mo, Muslin, $1 50.

Hannah More's complete Works.

With Engravings. 1 vol. 8vo, Sheep extra, $2 50 2 vols., $2 75.

Hannah More's complete Works.

Printed from large Type. 7 vols. royal 12mo, Muslin, $6 50.

Blunt's Ship-master's Assistant and

Commercial Digest: comprising Information necessary for Merchants, Owners, and Masters of Ships on the following Subjects: Masters, Mates, Seamen, Owners, Ships, Navigation Laws, Fisheries, Revenue Cutters, Custom House Laws, Importations, Clearing and Entering Vessels, Drawbacks, Freight, Insurance, Average, Salvage, Bottomry and Respondentia, Factors, Bills of Exchange, Exchange, Currencies, Weights, Measures, Wreck Laws, Quarantine Laws, Passenger Laws, Pilot Laws, Harbor Regulations, Marine Offenses, Slave Trade, Navy, Pensions, Consuls, Commercial Regulations of Foreign Nations. With an Appendix, containing the Tariff of the United States, and an Explanation of Sea Terms. 8vo, Sheep extra, $4 50.

Miss Edgeworth's Tales and Novels.

With Engravings. 10 vols. 12mo, Muslin. 75 cents per Volume. Sold separately or in Sets.

Mrs. Sherwood's Works.

With Engravings. 16 vols. 12mo, Muslin. 85 cents per Volume. Sold separately or in Sets.

Geor[illegible]ia Scenes.

V[illegible] original Illustrations. 12mo, Muslin, 90 cents

Neele's Literary Remains.

The Literary Remains of the late Henry Neele. 8vo, Muslin, $1 00.

Louis the Fourteenth, and the Court of

France in the Seventeenth Century. By Miss PARDOE. With numerous Engravings, Portraits, &c. 2 vols. 12mo, Muslin, $3 50.

Paulding's Letters from the South.

2 vols. 12mo, Muslin, $1 25.

Percy Anecdotes.

To which is added, a Selection of American Anecdotes. With Portraits. 8vo, Sheep extra, $2 00.

Prescott's Biographical and Critical

Miscellanies. Containing Notices of Charles Brockden Brown, the American Novelist.—Asylum for the Blind.—Irving's Conquest of Granada.—Cervantes.—Sir Walter Scott.—Chateaubriand's English Literature.—Bancroft's History of the United States.—Madame Calderon's Life in Mexico.—Molière.—Italian Narrative Poetry.—Poetry and Romance of the Italians.—Scottish Song.—Da Ponte's Observations. 8vo, Muslin, $2 00; Sheep extra, $2 25; half Calf, $2 50.

Pursuit of Knowledge under Difficulties;

its Pleasures and Rewards. Illustrated by Memoirs of eminent Men. 2 vols. 18mo, Muslin, 90 cents.

Pursuit of Knowledge under Difficulties;

its Pleasures and Rewards. Illustrated by Memoirs of eminent Men. Revised with Notes and a Preface, by Rev. Dr. WAYLAND, President of Brown University. With Portraits. 2 vols. 12mo, Muslin, $1 50.

Letters to Young Ladies.

By Mrs. L. H. SIGOURNEY. 12mo, Muslin, 90 cents Muslin, gilt edges, $1 00.

Letters to Mothers.

By Mrs. L. H. SIGOURNEY. 12mo, Muslin, 90 cents; Muslin, gilt edges, $1 00.

The Writings of Robert C. Sands.

With a Memoir. 2 vols. 8vo, Muslin, $3 75.

The Philosophy of Life, and Philosophy

of Language, in a Course of Lectures. By FREDERICK VON SCHLEGEL. Translated from the German, by the Rev. A. J. W. MORRISON, M.A. 12mo, Muslin, 90 cents.

Indian Tales and Legends;

Or, Algic Researches. Comprising Inquiries respecting the Mental Characteristics of the North American Indians. By HENRY R. SCHOOLCRAFT. 2 vols. 12mo, Muslin, $1 25.

Sismondi's Historical View of the Lit-

erature of the South of Europe. Translated, with Notes, by THOMAS ROSCOE. 2 vols. 12mo, Muslin, $1 80.

Hon. J. C. Smith's Correspondence and

Miscellanies. With an Eulogy pronounced before the Connecticut Historical Society at New Haven, May 27th, 1846, by the Rev. WILLIAM W. ANDREWS. 12mo, Muslin, $1 00.

The Doctor, &c.

By ROBERT SOUTHEY. 12mo, Muslin, 45 cents.

England and America:

A Comparison of the Social and Political State of both Nations. By E. G. WAKEFIELD. 8vo, Muslin, $1 25.

Mathews's Miscellaneous Writings:

Embracing The Motley Book, Behemoth, The Politicians, Poems on Man in the Republic, Wakondah, Puffer Hopkins, Miscellanies, Selections from Arcturus, International Copyright. 8vo, Muslin, $1 00.

Cassius M. Clay's Writings;

Including Speeches and Addresses. Edited, with a Preface and Memoir, by HORACE GREELEY. With a Portrait. 8vo, Muslin, $1 50.

Past and Present, Chartism, and Sartor

Resartus. By THOMAS CARLYLE. 12mo, Muslin, $1 00.

Letters of the British Spy.

By WILLIAM WIRT. To which is prefixed a Sketch of the Author's Life. 12mo, Muslin, 60 cents.

Raphael;

Or, Pages of the Book of Life at Twenty. By A. DE LAMARTINE. 12mo, Paper, 25 cents.

Verplanck's Right Moral Influence and

Use of Liberal Studies. 12mo, Muslin, 25 cents.

The Poems and Ballads of Schiller.

Translated by Sir E. BULWER LYTTON. With a brief Sketch of the Author's Life. 12mo, Muslin, 90 cents.

Longfellow's Poems.

A new Edition, enlarged by the Addition of "Evan geline." 8vo, Paper, 62½ cents.

Harper's Illustrated Shakespeare.

The complete Dramatic Writings of William Shakespeare, arranged according to recent approved collations of the Text; with Notes and other Illustrations by Hon. GULIAN C. VERPLANCK. Superbly Embellished by over 1400 exquisite Engravings by Hewet, after Designs by Meadows, Weir, and other eminent Artists. 3 vols royal 8vo, Muslin, $18 00; half Calf, $20 00; Turkey Morocco, gilt edges, $25 00.

Shakespeare's Dramatic Works.

With the Corrections and Illustrations of Dr. JOHNSON, G. STEEVENS, and others. Revised by ISAAC REED, Esq. With Engravings. 6 vols. royal 12mo Muslin $6 50.

Shakespeare's Dramatic Works and

Poems. With Notes, original and selected, and Introductory Remarks to each Play, by SAMUEL WELLER SINGER, and a Life of the Poet, by CHARLES SYMMONS, D.D. With Engravings. 8vo, Sheep extra 1 vol., $2 50; 2 vols., $2 75.

Cowper's Poetical Works.

With a Biographical and Critical Introduction, by the Rev. THOMAS DALE. With 75 Illustrations, engraved by E. Bookhout, from Drawings by John Gilbert. 2 vols. 8vo, Muslin, gilt edges, $3 75; Turkey Morocco, gilt edges, $5 00.

Milton's Poetical Works.

With a Memoir and Critical Remarks on his Genius and Writings, by JAMES MONTGOMERY. Illustrated by 120 Engravings, from Drawings by William Harvey. 2 vols. 8vo, Muslin, gilt edges, $3 75; imitation Morocco, gilt edges, $4 25; Turkey Morocco, gilt edges, $5 00.

Thomson's Seasons.

With engraved Illustrations by E. Bookhout, from Drawings on Wood by John Bell, Sculptor, C. W. Cope, Thomas Creswick, J. C. Horsley, J. P. Knight, A.R.A., R. Redgrave, A.R.A., Frank Stone, C. Stonhouse, Frederic Tayler, H. J. Townsend, and Thomas Webster, A.R.A. And with the Life of the Author, by PATRICK MURDOCH, D.D., F.R.S. Edited by BOLTON CORNEY, Esq. 8vo, Muslin, gilt edges, $2 75, imitation Morocco, gilt edges, $3 50; Turkey Morocco, gilt edges, $4 00.

Goldsmith's Poetical Works.

Illustrated by Wood Engravings from the Designs of C. W. Cope, Thomas Creswick, J. C. Horsley, R. Redgrave, and Frederic Tayler, Members of the Etching Club. With a Biographical Memoir, and Notes on the Poems. Edited by BOLTON CORNEY, Esq. 8vo, Muslin, gilt edges, $2 50; imitation Morocco, gilt edges, $3 25; Turkey Morocco, gilt edges, $3 75.

Bryant's Selections from American Poets.
18mo, Muslin, 45 cents.

Halleck's Selections from British Poets.
2 vols. 18mo, Muslin, 90 cents.

Alnwick Castle,
And other Poems. By FITZ-GREENE HALLECK, Esq. 12mo, Muslin, $1 12½.

Fanny,
And other Poems. By FITZ-GREENE HALLECK, Esq. With Vignette. 12mo, Muslin, $1 12½.

Hoffman's Poems.
18mo, Paper, 25 cents; Muslin, 50 cents.

Model Men, Women, and Children.
By HORACE MAYHEW. With numerous Illustrations. 18mo, Muslin, 62½ cents.

Hart's Romance of Yachting.
Voyage the First. 12mo, Paper, 75 cents; Muslin, $1 00.

Home Influence:
A Tale for Mothers and Daughters. By GRACE AGUILAR. 12mo, Paper, 75 cents; Muslin, $1 00.

Thankfulness.
A Narrative. Comprising Passages from the Diary of the Rev. Allan Temple. By the Rev. C. B. TAYLER. 12mo, Paper, 37½ cents; Muslin, 50 cents.

Old Hicks the Guide;
Or, Adventures in the Camanche Country in search of a Gold Mine. By CHARLES WEBBER. 12mo, Paper, 75 cents; Muslin, $1 00.

The Children of the New Forest.
A Novel. By Captain MARRYAT. 12mo, Paper, 37½ cents; Muslin 50 cents.

Charles the First.

We incline to think that there never was before so much said about this unfortunate monarch in so short a space; so much to the purpose with so much impartiality; and in such a style as just suits those for whom it is designed—the "two millions" of young persons in the United States, who ought to be supplied with such works as these. The engravings represent the prominent persons and places of the history, and are well executed. The portrait of John Hampden is charming. The antique title-page is rich.—*Southern Christian Advocate.*

Hannibal the Carthaginian.

A new volume of the series projected by the skillful book-manufacturer, Mr. Abbott, who displays no little tact in engaging the attention of that marvellous body "the reading public" in old scholastic topics hitherto almost exclusively the property of the learned. The latter, with their ingenious implements of lexicons and scholia, will be in no danger of being superseded, however, while the least-furnished reader may gain something from the attractively-printed and easily-perused volumes of Mr. Abbott. The story of Hannibal is well adapted for popular treatment, and loses nothing for this purpose in the present explanatory and pictorial version.—*Literary World.*

Maria Antoinette.

In a style copious and yet forcible, with an expression singularly clear and happy, and in language exceedingly chaste and at times very beautiful, he has given us a plain, unvarnished narrative of facts, as he himself says, unclogged by individual reflections which would "only encumber rather than enforce." The present work wants none of the interest inseparably connecting itself with the preceding numbers of the same series, but is characterized throughout by the same peculiar beauties, riveting the attention and deeply engraving on the mind the information with which they every where teem.—*Evening Mirror.*

Alexander the Great.

The history of Alexander the Great, as penned by Jacob Abbott, will be read with thrilling interest. It is profusely embellished, containing maps of the Expedition of Alexander, of Macedon and Greece, the plain of Troy, the Granicus, and the plain of Issus; and engravings of Alexander and Bucephalus; Paris and Helen; the bathing in the river Cyndus; the siege of Tyre; Alexander at the siege of Susa; and the proposed improvement of Mount Athos. It is written in a most graphic and attractive style.—*Spectator.*

Charles the Second.

A valuable engraving of Lely's portrait of Cromwell opens the book, and there are several illustrative wood engravings and an illuminated title-page. This is a comprehensive and simple narration of the main features of the period during which Charles the Second reigned, and it is done with the clear scope and finely-written style which would be expected from the pen of Jacob Abbott—one of the most able and useful literary men, as he is one of the very best teachers of his time.—*Home Journal.*

Julius Cæsar.

The author seems gifted with that peculiar faculty, possessed by so few, of holding communion with and drawing out ardent imagination and budding genius, and at the same time of directing both into the great channel of truth. The labors of such a man are productive of incalculable good, and deserve the highest reward.—*New Hampshire Patriot*

Richard the First.

Mr. Abbott's entertaining and instructive historical works are becoming more and more popular, and are undoubtedly among the best of the many condensed histories that have been written. For young people we know of nothing more entertaining or better calculated to excite a desire to become acquainted with the leading events of history.—*Buffalo Cour*

Richard the Third.

We know of no writer in this country whose style and ability bettei fit him for such a service. They are admirable works for youth, and make a valuable fund of reading for the fireside and for schoc.s.—*New York Evangelist.*

Alfred the Great.

History, under the pen of Mr. Abbott, discloses its narratives and utters its lessons in a style of great simplicity and intelligence, and, above all, with no danger of detriment to morals. He has selected his field with excellent taste, and we shall be glad to see his series pursued indefinitely. In their line, these volumes have never been surpassed.—*Bavtist Recorder.*

Darius, King of Persia.

Mr. Abbott's design to write a succession of histories for the young is admirable, and worthy of all encouragement, and the manner in which he has executed his work thus far is most excellent. Let him be encouraged to proceed till he has reached the last volume of history, that the coming generation may turn from the world of romance to that of reality, and learn that what is and has been is as brilliant in character, as glorious in description, and as captivating in detail, as that which the genius of fiction ever created.—*Observer.*

William the Conqueror.

These historical memoirs by Mr. Abbott are marked by their great impartiality, condensation of facts and picturesqueness of style; his practiced and elegant pen has, in *Mary Queen of Scots* and *Charles the First*, invested the historic page with the brilliancy and fascination of romance.—*Mirror*

Xerxes the Great.

"The grand excellence of these little volumes is, that those points of history which involve the principles, the causes of human action, and which too often receive but little attention from those who write for youth, are brought forward into their proper station and so successfully treated, that the weakest capacities may become interested and stronger ones profited. The maps and engravings, of which there are many, add much to their value."

KINGS AND QUEENS;

OR, LIFE IN THE PALACE: CONSISTING OF HISTORICAL SKETCHES OF JOSEPHINE AND MARIA LOUISA, LOUIS PHILIPPE, FERDINAND OF AUSTRIA, NICHOLAS, ISABELLA II., LEOPOLD, AND VICTORIA.

BY JOHN S. C. ABBOTT.

With numerous Illustrations. 12*mo*, *Muslin*, $1 00.

These sketches of the most distinguished personages of Europe are drawn by a master hand, and with the life-like distinctness which characterizes all the works of the popular author. The work is full of romantic interest, while at the same time its perusal will enable the reader to understand the present state of Europe and of the crowned heads who form an essential part of its shifting pageantry.—*Ladies' Wreath.*

Brief, but very comprehensive and glowing sketches of eminent sovereigns are comprised in this beautiful little volume. The present political posture of some of these characters, and the wonderful incidents connected with others, give this work almost the air of a romance, so eventful, stirring, and unexpected is the history of their lives and fortunes. The views of Mr. Abbott are those of a thoughtful, conscientious, well-read man; and are far more trustworthy, to those who desire to know the real truth of history, than the representations of many historians who pass for standard authors.—*Evangelist.*

www.ingramcontent.com/pod-product-compliance
Lightning Source LLC
LaVergne TN
LVHW010221110826
845151LV00004B/1162

* 9 7 8 1 4 2 5 5 2 7 6 2 4 *